A HISTORY OF THE IRISH CHURCH 400 – 700AD

A History
of the Irish Church
400 – 700 AD

John R. Walsh
Thomas Bradley

the columba press

First Edition 1991
THE COLUMBA PRESS
93 The Rise, Mount Merrion, Blackrock, Co Dublin

Second, revised edition 1993

Designed by Bill Bolger
Origination by The Columba Press
Printed in Ireland by
Genprint Ltd., Dublin

ISBN: 1 85607 020 4

Maps

The maps throughout are designed by Bill Bolger. The contents of three of them are derived from previously published maps: that on page 27 from *Irish Kings and High-Kings*, by Francis John Byrne (Batsford, London, 1973); that on page 43 from *Ireland before the Vikings*, by Gearóid MacNiocaill (Gill & Macmillan, 1972); and that on page 89 from *The Celtic Churches: A History, AD 200–1200*, by John J McNeill (University of Chicago Press, 1974).

Photographs

The illustrations on the cover and on pages 57, 105, 115, 131 & 141 are used by courtesy of The Office of Public Works, Dublin; those on pages 145 & 147 by courtesy of Trinity College, Dublin; that on page 49 by courtesy of the National Museum, Dublin, and that on page 33 by courtesy of the Northern Ireland Tourist Board.

Contents

Dedicated to our pupils, past and present
Would that you might aim at greater and better!
[Confessio, 47]

Foreword

The idea of writing this book first originated many years ago – when one of us was a teacher and the other a pupil. By the time we became colleagues, the groundwork had been done and the school could boast of an extensive library on the Celtic Church. It is to the generations of authors whose works are represented in this collection that we are chiefly indebted. These scholars, in books or learned articles, have grappled with countless problems associated with the period. We acknowledge our debt to these scholars in the main body of the text and in our bibliography. We say little that is new in this volume but we hope that we have been able to produce a synthesis and to provide a pathway through the maze that confronts the reader of early Irish ecclesiastical history.

We have been given much help and advice by teaching colleagues. In particular, we thank Brian McGoldrick for his many keen insights and invaluable comments. We are grateful to Danny Gorman and Seán McMahon who did so much to improve the readability of the work. Within the school also, our resource technician George Gillen was always prepared to carry out unreasonable demands with characteristic alacrity and Harry Doherty contributed his expertise on the word processor. Above all, we cannot forget our pupils who were the main source of inspiration. Their acute comments and probing questions were a constant stimulus. We dedicate this *libellus* to them.

We were greatly assisted in our researches by three friends: Maurice Healy proved a relentless sleuth in Belfast libraries; Kieran Devlin shared his knowledge of the period and his mastery of our native tongue; and Oliver Crilly made constructive suggestions, particularly with reference to the contents of Chapter Twelve, and emboldened us with his unrivalled familiarity with the Dublin publishing world.

Without the generosity – and the deadlines – of our publisher, this book would not have happened. Seán O Boyle of Columba Press has a deep personal interest in our subject. The warmth and enthusiasm of his reaction to our overtures, when we approached him to publish the tome, made our efforts over the years worthwhile.

Finally, we applaud our respective families for their forbearance and encouragement. For what they regarded as a worthy endeavour they were willing to put up with absences and preoccupations which, had the situation been reversed, we might not have accepted so graciously.

J.R.W. and T.B.,
St Columb's College,
Derry.
6th November 1990
The Feast of All the Saints of Ireland.

Foreword to the Second Edition

Since its publication, readers have been good enough to send us corrections of errors in the first edition. These emendations have now been incorporated. The bibliography has been updated somewhat.

J.R.W. and T.B.
St Columb's College
Derry.
9th June 1993
The Feast of St Colum Cille

CHAPTER ONE

Pre-Patrician Christianity

He is coming, Adzed-Head,
on the wild-headed sea
with cloak hollow-headed
and curve-headed staff.

He will chant false religion
at a bench facing east
and his people will answer
'Amen, amen.'

[Anonymous sixth-century
Hiberno-Latin poem;
quoted by Muirchú]

Traditionally, the humble Saint Patrick has been credited with converting the entire Irish race from paganism in the very short period between 432 and 461. It would be romantic and even gratifying if this were indeed the case. Sobering though it is, however, we have to admit that there were certainly Christians in Ireland before Patrick arrived as a missionary in the country and that the saint worked as an evangelist only in a part of the island.

Christianity entered Ireland, presumably in the fourth and early fifth centuries, by a slow and gradual process of unplanned infiltration, from the continent (Gaul and perhaps even the Iberian peninsula) and/or Britain. British captives carried off by Irish raiders are one possible means of entry; contacts made by the Irish *emigrés* in Britain are another; and trade relations with Gaul, Roman Britain or Spain are yet another. Some continental *literati* may even have sought refuge in Ireland during the barbarian invasions of what is now France, at the start of the fifth century, bringing their Christian religion with them.

As we approach the end of the twentieth century, the communications era *par excellence*, we are so familiar with high-speed trains,

1

chartered flights and scheduled airlines that our world is, indeed, a 'global village'. It is possible nowadays to breakfast at home in Ireland and to sit down to lunch on the same day three thousand miles away in New York! Because of this we assume that our early ancestors were totally cut off from the outside world by the cruel seas which surround our island, that they were completely isolated and most insular. This is not an accurate picture of life in ancient times. In fact, the sea then united rather than divided peoples on the whole Atlantic seaboard of Europe in what modern historians, like E G Bowen, call 'a Celtic thalassocracy', and the waters from Malin Head and Cape Wrath to Finisterre and beyond were a hive of maritime activity.

Our ancient mariners sailed in curraghs, wooden-framed craft covered in hides and capable of negotiating stormy seas with agility and in safety. Irish boats of similar (though somewhat later) construction were, we know, able to reach Iceland, a journey of about a thousand miles, within six days! We learn from Giraldus Cambrensis that in 1185 Ireland was considered 'about one short day's sailing from Wales', half a day's journey across the North Channel 'between Ulster and Galloway in Scotland', and 'three ordinary days' sailing' from Spain. In the twelfth century, vessels were, of course, more sophisticated than the early coracles. But even in the period before Christ some tiny sailing boats had been given rudders and other navigational aids. The delightful little model ship, part of the Broighter gold hoard (of Co Derry provenance) in the National Museum, shows how large these sea-going vessels could be. It has nine benches for eighteen oarsmen in all, a rudder, a mast, three booms, a punting pole and an anchor. In seaworthy craft such as this, our proto-historic Celtic ancestors plied the seas, searching for places on which to prey, in which to settle or with which to trade.

The primitive Irish were expert plunderers. We know, for example, that Patrick was captured in a great raid which netted 'many thousands of people' [*Confessio* 1], some of them, at least, lukewarm Christians, according to Patrick's pessimistic diagnosis of their common spiritual condition. Doubtless a number of his fellow captives would actually have been committed Christians and a few may, indeed, even have been priests. Doubtless, too, as Gildas (c 500-570) informs us, this was not the only raid made on Britain by the *grassatores Hiberni* ('the Irish thugs'). One local king, Niall Noígiallach ('of the Nine Hostages'), the son of a ruler with the soubriquet 'Lord of the Slaves' and a woman who was herself probably a British slave-girl, is said to have made seven marauding expeditions across the Irish Sea. Looted Roman coins have been found in abundance all along the northern

PRE-PATRICIAN CHRISTIANITY

and eastern coasts of Ireland: at the Giant's Causeway in 1831; at Coleraine in 1854; and in much more recent times at Limavady, Co Derry, for instance. The advent of Christian slaves, then, possibly played a part in the introduction of Christianity into the island. And, since rulers in a country could obviously acquire the most slaves, it follows that enslaved Christians might well have had access to the most influential people in the land of their captivity.

The ancient Irish were expansionists. From the end of the third century onwards the *Scotti*, as the inhabitants of Ireland were generally called, established a number of colonies on the island of Great Britain: in north-western and south-western Wales, Cornwall and western Scotland {Note 1}. Intercourse between these immigrants and Christian Britons and members of the Roman imperial forces could possibly have led to the conversion of some of them and ultimately to a haphazard spread of the faith to Ireland; particularly to the south and east coasts opposite the settlements in Wales and Cornwall.

The Irish had strong trading links with Roman Britain and Gaul and some dealings with Iberia {Note 2}. While they were unfamiliar with 'the interior parts' of the island, Tacitus (c 55-120 A D) tells us that British or Gallic merchants had a reasonably good knowledge of Ireland's 'harbours and approaches' and there is good evidence that Roman traders reached not just the coastal harbours but points well inland along large rivers like the Nore and the Barrow. It seems that wine and oil (and possibly wheat) were carried in considerable quantities from the continent to Ireland. Archaeologists have discovered ample evidence of a wine trade, especially in the south of the country. It is probably no coincidence that the Corcu Loegde of the modern west Cork, who later claimed to be the first Irish Christians, carried on an extensive wine-trade with France. It is interesting to note, also, that the word *Bordgal*, the Archaic Old Irish form of the place-name *Bordeaux*, is to be found in the toponymy of Westmeath and Kilkenny, and is also a word in Goidelic meaning 'meeting-place'. The Irish also imported pottery, metal-work and bric-à-brac from Roman Gaul and Britain. In exchange for these commodities they exported copper and gold, slaves, hides, cattle and wolfhounds. While evangelisation is not the primary motive of the commercial traveller, and while French wine-shippers were doubtless more intent on filling Irish stomachs with liquor than Irish souls with religion, it is possible that foreign merchants used the opportunities afforded by their business contacts to interest some Irish people in Christianity {Note 3}.

It is a distinct possibility that some Christian 'learned men' fled to Ireland during the invasion of Gaul by German-speaking peoples at the beginning of the fifth century. The *Leiden Glossary*, a twelfth-century document based on a sixth or seventh-century account written in Gaul but now lost, claims that such a migration took place: 'All the learned men on this side of the sea took flight, and in transmarine parts, namely in Ireland and wherever they betook themselves, brought about a very great increase of learning to the inhabitants of those regions.' That civilised men would have fled to Ireland in fear of barbarian invaders is not beyond belief. The island would thus have gained from the ill-wind that blew across the continent, and would have become the recipient of whatever body of knowledge these men possessed. These Gallic *literati* would probably have maintained their identity for a considerable period of time among the pagan Irish. Patrick's mention of 'rhetoricians' [*Confessio* 13] may be a reference to these scholarly fugitives.

It seems, too, that that obscure product of a very sophisticated but Christian environment, the *Hisperica Famina* (*Western Sayings*) may have been penned by seventh-century scholars in Ireland from this particular background. Modern authorities widely believe that the *Western Sayings* is of Irish origin and probably from a monastic environment. An examination of the contents of the document reinforces speculation that it originated in Ireland as it portrays a country where the natives communicate in Irish. The work is in strange, esoteric and unfamiliar language and gives the appearance of having been composed as a lesson-book for students of advanced Latin. Its vocabulary is most strikingly indebted to Isidore of Saville (c 560-636), but it also bears a vague resemblance to the *Altus Prosator* (called in English *Ancient of Days*), a poem attributed to Columba, and to some of the writings of Columban. James F Kenney suggests that this famous work may have been produced in Ireland by descendants of the early fifth-century, fugitive Gallic men of letters mentioned in the *Leiden Glossary* {Note 4}.

One, some or all of the avenues detailed above may have brought Christianity into Ireland. Of its presence in the country by the start of the fifth century we can be in no doubt for there is indisputable, mainly cumulative, evidence that Christianity had reached Ireland before Patrick began his mission in 432 {Note 5}.

Linguistic studies are of assistance in attempting to throw light on the progress of Christianity in early Celtic Ireland. The history of certain British words derived from Latin and borrowed by Archaic Old Irish, such as *Cáisc* ('Easter') and *cruimther* ('priest'), suggests the gradual conversion of Ireland by Britons in the fourth and possibly early fifth centuries. These words reveal a most basic practice of the faith in an undeveloped Church without a bishop, for there is no word in rudimentary Old Irish for 'bishop'. The first stratum of Christian loan-words is therefore possibly pre-431 when 'the first bishop' arrived in the country. The improvised vocabulary of the nascent Irish Church came into Archaic Old Irish through British speech rather than directly from Latin. It follows from this that British Christians, or their Irish converts on their return home, introduced these loan-words (and probably the faith they reflected) into parts of the island {Note 6}.

There is a tradition, too, that certain Irish saints preceded Saint Patrick in date: notably Ciaran of Saiger, Declan of Ardmore, Ibar of Beccére, Ailbe of Emly, M'eltioc of Kinsale, Mo-chanoc and Mo-chatoc. The *Lives* of these saints are all very late – no earlier than the twelfth century – and provide no conclusive evidence that they were active in the pre-Patrician period. Most of these were probably British by birth, to judge by their names, and most are associated with the south and the south-east of the country. This, and other evidence available to him, leads Thomas F O'Rahilly to make the sweeping claims that 'Irish Christianity owes its origin to Britain', that 'already before 431 no small part of the population of the south-east and south of Ireland must have been converted by British missionaries', that British evangelists continued to arrive in Ireland during the next three decades, and that after 461 British influence had the field to itself. Nor does the dearth of evidence prevent E A Thompson from basing his account of Patrick's activity in Ireland on the supposition that British Christians resident in Ireland formed the nucleus round which he established his Church in Ireland. All we can say with confidence is that British Christians, either directly or indirectly, influenced the spread of the faith to Ireland and that this influence may have been exerted before 431.

James F Kenney is of the opinion that another ground for concluding that there were Christians in Ireland prior to Patrick's mission is that there are traces in Ireland of certain heresies – Arianism, Priscillianism and Pelagianism – which were current in western Europe in the late fourth and early fifth centuries. It is even possible that some of Priscillian's adherents made their way to Ireland after their leader's execution in 386. Pelagius (355-425) was responsible for much doctrinal controversy in the Church in the opening decades of the fifth century. He denied the necessity of grace for salvation and emphasised instead God's gift of free will to men. Pelagius was certainly a most articulate and highly influential individual in his generation. This celebrated figure may have been an Irishman, for his adversary Saint Jerome vilifies him as a 'most stupid fellow, heavy with Irish porridge' and claims that he, or his companion Coelestius, had 'his lineage of the Irish race, from the neighbourhood of the Britons.' It is more likely that Jerome was merely insulting his opponent in the way we might dismiss another as a 'Philistine'. Pelagius received his training, spent his life and made his real impact on the continent. It would be foolhardy, then, to accept the dubious evidence regarding his origins and to claim that he was representative of a flourishing, if deviant, Irish Church. The only conclusions that can be reached are either that these heresies infected pre-Patrician Christians in Ireland or that the traces remain from a later contamination. Pelagius definitely had a pernicious effect on the Church in Roman Britain and it was to combat this threat that Germanus of Auxerre was sent by Rome to that island in 429. An offshoot of this excursion was the subsequent mission of the 'first bishop', Palladius, 'to the *Scotti* who believe in Christ': incontrovertible evidence that from at least the third decade of the fifth century, there were sufficient Irish Christians to justify the appointment of a bishop for them by Rome {Note 7}.

431 is regarded as the first unassailable date in Irish history. Under that year Prosper of Aquitaine entered in his *Chronicon* (*Chronicle*) the words: 'Palladius, ordained by Pope Celestine, is sent to the *Scotti* who believe in Christ, as their first bishop.' Palladius, probably a deacon of Auxerre at the time of his elevation, is the man referred to above as having been instrumental in having Germanus sent to tackle Pelagianism in Britain. James Carney claims that Prosper 'used *Scotti* in a restricted sense and intended to refer geographically not to Ireland but to Scotland.' He states that a number of church-dedications to Saint Paldy in southern Scotland seem to attest his presence there but he is convinced that there is no evidence of Palladius having been in Ireland. It is most likely that Carney is wrong in this conjecture for Dál Riata, the Scottic colony in what is now Argyll, was probably founded only in the final years of the fifth century. Furthermore most modern scholars definitely associate Palladius with hallowed spots in Leinster.

Thankfully, Prosper gives us another small item of information which throws some light on the matter. In his *Contra Collatorem* (*Against the Contributor*), written about 434 in Rome, Prosper seems to imply that Palladius's mission was to Ireland itself. He writes of his master Pope Celestine: 'By ordaining a bishop for the *Scotti*, while he strove to keep the Roman island Catholic he also made the barbarous island Christian.' Most scholars accept that this gives proof positive that Palladius's mission was to Ireland, 'the barbarous island', itself and that the Pope managed also to preserve Britain, 'the Roman island', from the Pelagian heresy by sending Germanus of Auxerre there in 429. Undaunted, Carney argues that Britain was metaphorically 'divided into two "islands", the northern barbaric, the southern Roman, and we are not merely entitled, but compelled, to dissociate Palladius from Ireland.' His theory is based on the fact that all of Britain had not been subjugated by the Romans and that the north had remained unconquered and pagan.

Nevertheless, most authorities remain unconvinced by Carney's ingenious theory and believe that Palladius laboured, for some time at least, unobtrusively in Ireland. The fact that Muirchú, in his seventh-century *Life*, makes Patrick the successor of Palladius adds strength to their position. Muirchú states: 'They knew for certain that Palladius ... had been consecrated and sent to this island in the cold north in order to convert it ... Neither were these wild and harsh men inclined to accept his teaching nor did he himself wish to spend a long time in a foreign country, but decided to return to him [Pope Celestine] who had sent him. On his way back from here, having crossed the first sea and begun his journey by land, he ended his life in the territory of the Britons' [I,8]. Thomas F O'Rahilly argues quite brilliantly that the activities of Palladius and Patrick have become confused and that much of the work of Palladius, who, he claims, was called *Patricius* in Ireland, has been wrongly attributed to Patrick. He believes that Palladius laboured in Ireland until 461 and was then succeeded by Patrick who worked there until his death about 492. Most Patrician scholars of this century do not make such exaggerated claims. John Ryan [1931] holds that the first bishop's mission in Ireland was short and that 'within a year Palladius was dead.' Ludwig Bieler [1967] suggests that Palladius was 'still successfully active in Ireland at least two or three years after his commission' at the time (434) of Prosper's entry in his *Against the Contributor*. Bieler holds that Palladius laboured in the south-eastern corner of the island. He observes that a bishop sent by Rome would have had the assistance of quite a large staff and that a mission with papal backing would have been constantly reinforced by fresh personnel.

Something like this may indeed have happened. Palladius could have established a church in Leinster, with his work being continued by shadowy figures like Secundinus, Auxilius and Iserninus – men who had no contact whatsoever with Patrick. Professor Corish, in his recent most incisive study, *The Irish Catholic Experience* (Dublin, 1985), builds on the case put forward so cogently by D A Binchy in 1962. Corish speculates that 'the fragments of topographical information that cling to Palladius's name locate his mission in Leinster' (actually with three very ancient churches in Co Wicklow) and that his efforts were supplemented or continued in that general area by the missionaries named above. Auxilius and Iserninus are credited, along with Patrick, with issuing the circular letter known as *The First Synod of Saint Patrick*. Monsignor Corish has no difficulty in associating the canons in this particular document with Auxilius and Iserninus. Kathleen Hughes [1966] is of the opinion that the document was produced by a fairly well-developed, second-generation yet still missionary Church in Leinster. The venerable Church of Kildare, still strong enough in the seventh century to be regarded as a rival of Armagh, may, we might add, have then been a relic of the former effectiveness and independence of the fifth-century Roman mission of Palladius and his followers in Leinster. Corish believes that Patrick played no part in the framing of the document which now bears his name and that it 'is not hard to see circumstances in which his name came to be added later.'

In his *Confessio* [51], Patrick shows himself aware of episcopal activity elsewhere in Ireland and the administration (independently of him) of the sacraments of baptism, confirmation and ordination. He states that he himself had travelled to places in Ireland 'where no-one else had ever penetrated, in order to baptise, or to ordain clergy, or to confirm the people' – thus insinuating that there were, indeed, places in the country which had received spiritual ministrations from another (possibly earlier) source or indeed other sources. Furthermore, his account of his flight from slavery as a young man of twenty-two may give evidence of an escape network for fugitive slaves run by concerned Christians, presumably in Leinster, more than twenty years before Patrick began his own mission [*Confessio* 17 and 18]. But Patrick does not refer to Palladius or any other missionary, predecessor or contemporary, by name. One of Patrick's outstanding traits is his humility. If Palladius's mission was anything other than unspectacular (and probably short) it is difficult to imagine that Patrick would not have acknowledged the fact. He clearly regarded himself as essentially a pioneer, and not as anybody's successor or co-operator. Though the Palladian and Patrician missions may have coincided, Patrick was working in virgin territory bringing the Gospel to pagans, whereas the Roman missionaries in Leinster were consolidating the work done by Palladius and begun by the anonymous evangelists who, by 431, had ensured that there was no small number of *Scotti* believing in Christ.

The record of the coming of Christianity into Ireland is obscure and even confusing. It cannot be denied, however, that the faith had already taken root in the island before the mission of Saint Patrick, apostle of Ireland. How the new religion established itself in the country is a hazy yet tantalising chapter in our early history. By the time the saint had begun his mission, the groundwork had been done and the foundations had been laid for a Celtic Church in Ireland that over the next few centuries would become one of the most vibrant parts of the Body of Christ.

Notes:

1. Though the settlement in Argyll in Scotland probably dates from the closing years of the fifth century and has, therefore, questionable relevance for the topic under discussion, we mention it to underline the extent of Irish colonial activity in Britain in our period. For a fresh treatment of Irish *emigrés* in Britain, see Lloyd and Jennifer Laing, *Celtic Britain and Ireland, AD 200-800: The Myth of the Dark Ages* (Blackrock, Co Dublin, 1990).

2. Art historians have discovered links between specialised motifs, notably the Visigothic marigold design, on artifacts in the Iberian peninsula and in Ireland. These supposed associations are confirmed (or at least supported) by references in the writings of Orosius, the early fifth-century Portuguese historian and apologist, to a special relationship between Galicia, the Celtic settlement in Spain, and Ireland. (It is interesting to remember, as supportive evidence of the strength and endurance of this interrelationship, the existence of a very early Celtic monastery with Irish connections, prior to the Arab conquest of Spain in the seventh century, at Santa Maria de Bretoña near Mondoñedo in the same region.)

3. It is surely significant that the earliest stratum of Latin loan-words in Archaic Old Irish is concerned with the vocabulary of mercantile activity.

4. The earliest form of writing in Ireland, the Ogham Script, is based on the Latin alphabet and is most commonly found on standing-stones in Kerry, Cork and Waterford, the very region where these French scholars are thought to have settled. While these erudite *emigrés* did not import the art of writing into Ireland (for Ogham Script may have been introduced as early as the fourth century), they were coming to a country already touched by Roman scholarship and open to deeper influences.

5. We can, of course, dismiss the four pious legends which make an Irishman: (1) a witness (Altus) to the events on Calvary; (2) a ruler in Ulster (Conor Mac Nessa) who died broken-hearted on hearing of Christ's crucifixion; (3) an important local king (Cormac Mac Airt) who converted in the third century; and (4) a bishop (Mansuetus) in fourth-century France.

6. The cults of two prominent saints, one from France and the other from Britain, were also imported into the country. Early Irish Christians venerated Saint Martin of Tours and Saint Ninian, the founder of *Candida Casa*, the famous early monastery on the west coast of northern Britain. There are the ancient parishes of Desertmartin (Co Derry) and Templemartin (Co Cork) and a townland called Kilmartin (Co Dublin), for example, and Ninian features in many of the early martyrologies. These cults may have been introduced by Gallic and Brittonic evangelists in the decades before Patrick's mission. However, it is more likely that they reflect a later devotion to Martin or Ninian among Irish Christians who had connections with Gaul or northern Britain.

7. The reader will find translations (with notes and explanations) of pertinent texts, written in Latin in the fourth and fifth centuries, in Liam de Paor, *Saint Patrick's World* (Blackrock, Co Dublin, 1993).

Patrick: The Man

*'Although I am imperfect
in many respects,
I wish my brethren and relatives
to know my disposition,
so that they may be able
to understand the aspirations
of my soul ...
I was like a stone
lying in deep mud;
and He who is mighty came,
and in His own mercy raised me
and lifted me up, and placed me
at the very top of the wall.'*

[*Confessio* 6 and 12]

Saint Patrick is at the 'very top of the wall' that forms the Irish Church and yet the historical Patrick is in many ways inaccessible to us in the twentieth century, buried as he is under the 'deep mud' that centuries of lore and legend have heaped on top of him. It is necessary to excavate this mire if we are to uncover the real Saint Patrick.

This study of Patrick's background, early career, character and convictions concentrates on the only sources likely to be truly informed about him: the *Confessio* (*Confession*) and the *Epistola* (*Letter*), two documents penned by the saint himself {Note 1}. Few scholars today question the authenticity of these two works. And the Latin is so poor, the style so obscure and the content so self-depreciatory that no one would have wished to compose these works and then attribute them to Patrick. Even though they were not intended to be auto-biographical, it is to his own writings that we turn in an attempt to seek reliable information about Patrick: to discover, for instance, where and when he was born, the location and duration of his captivity in Ireland, the dates and extent of his mission, the whereabouts of his vocational formation (for which reference shall have to be made to one of the *Sayings* attributed to the saint) and what we can of the man's personality and ideals. It may be worthwhile, however, to examine in some detail all the documents that can be positively or at least fairly confidently ascribed to Patrick.

The first-mentioned document gets its name from a sentence in its final chapter: 'This is my confession before I die.' The work was therefore composed towards the end of its author's life and when he was sixty years or upwards (*in senectute mea* – 'in my old age') [10]. Comprising sixty-two chapters in all, it is a defence of the saint's mission in Ireland and of his methods, attitudes and lifestyle there. Patrick had been subjected to adverse criticism from church people in Britain and opponents in Ireland. He was accused of being ill-educated, blundering, arrogant, self-seeking and even sinful – unworthy of the episco pal office of which he was so proud.

In response to these accusations, Patrick asserts that his was a God-given vocation and that God assisted him throughout his life. To support this claim he refers to several visions or dreams which he had experienced – proof of God's intervention on his behalf and of God's approval of what the saint had tried to accomplish. The work is written in crude and often incoherent Latin and is frustratingly ambiguous and sometimes unintelligible. Any direct references to the writer's background and active ministry are few and merely incidental. The *Confessio* was drawn up in Ireland for 'those who believe in and fear God' [62], but especially for the clerical members of his retinue, his critics in Ireland and Britain, his own blood-relations and his ecclesiastical friends in his native land. Patrick's *Confessio* has at least three major themes: an admission of his worldly and indeed sinful youth; an expression of praise and thanks to God for God's direction and use of Patrick; and a defence of his mission and conduct in Ireland in the face of innuendo and criticism.

The *Epistola* probably predates the *Confessio*. Consisting of twenty-one brief chapters, it resembles the longer document in thought and language but, written in a burst of energy, in extreme but controlled indignation, it is much more coherent. Its composition was occasioned by a raid made by a British prince Coroticus, a potentate in Strathclyde or Wales or an outlaw in northern Ireland, and his soldiers upon a group of Patrick's neophytes in Ireland. These marauders may have been associated with Irishmen or 'apostate' [2] Picts. The raiders killed many of the new converts and carried others off into slavery, taking with them also a large booty. Patrick's letter of protest is directed primarily at clerical subjects of the despot but is also addressed to Coroticus himself, to the cruel ruler's errant soldiers and to Christians in general in the territory under his control. The document has the same defensive and self-justificatory tone as the *Confessio*. Patrick's main themes in this work are: a denunciation of the attack by nominal Christians upon fellow Christians; concern for the fate of the captives; a demand for the excommunication of the perpetrators of the deed; and a plea for repentance by 'Coroticus and his guilty minions' [19].

The *First Synod of Saint Patrick* and the *Dicta Patricii* (*Sayings of Patrick*) purport to be from the pen or lips of the saint. Crucial for an appreciation of Patrician chronology and of the significance of the Palladian mission, the former is an open letter to the clergy of Ireland by (supposedly) the bishops Patrick, Auxilius and Iserninus. It is the earliest extant work concerning ecclesiastical discipline in Ireland and details canons which the bishops had drawn up and are now promulgating. Bury and Bieler [1963] argue for the substantial authenticity of these canons, the latter even venturing a date (457) for the synod where they were drafted. Initially, Binchy [1962] argued that the canons were drawn up in seventh-century Ireland but later became convinced that the document 'really belongs to the sixth century'. Binchy [1968] was persuaded to this second position by Kathleen Hughes [1966] who argues strongly for a mid-sixth century date for the main bulk of this legislation, claiming that the canons depict a fairly well-developed Church rather than a first-generation missionary one, but a Church co-existing, albeit reluctantly, with vigorous paganism. Hughes holds that these canons must therefore be considerably later than the Church of Patrick. We find the approach of Monsignor Corish to the dating of this document particularly attractive and are happy to view the canons not as the work of Patrick but as the product of Auxilius and Iserninus and their mid-fifth century, second-generation yet still missionary, Palladian Church in Leinster.

The three so-called *Sayings of Patrick* {Note 2} are very important. The first one is especially so, for on it hangs the case for Patrick's supposed continental associations. Bieler [1967] is inclined to accept the authenticity of the first *Dictum* and, at least, part of the third. The second, since it is a brief extract from the *Epistola*, is certainly Patrician but it adds nothing to our knowledge of the saint. Bishop Hanson [1983] dismisses the first and third *Dicta* as belonging to an age later than Patrick's.

What then do our sources tell us about Patrick? The saint was born in Roman Britain. His father, Calpornius, was a decurion, a hereditary alderman, one of the municipal officials in a lesser local government area, or *vicus*, entrusted with the task of collecting taxes for the central Roman administration. The law made decurions liable, among other things, for the debts of tax-evaders. It was an expensive honour, therefore, and one which many tried to avoid. One way of escaping the burden of such an office was to enter holy orders. Ordination gave a man tax-exemption and, in hard times, provided the Church with propertied, educated ecclesiastics, who would have had administrative experience. The practice was therefore mutually beneficial to the Church and to the ordinand and so it was quite common in the fourth century to find men who held the office of decurion escaping the obligations of their rank by seeking ordination. Patrick's father and grandfather would appear to have done this: Calpornius was a deacon and the son of Potitus, a priest.

Patrick tells us that his father ministered in the *vicus* [*Confessio* 1] of *Bannavem Taberniae*, near which he had a small estate. But we cannot be sure if this is where he himself was born. Nor can we be certain that the placename as we now have it is the name the *vicus* had in Patrick's youth for perhaps the original name was *Bannaventa Berniae* and a later copyist has been guilty of an error in transcription. All we know is that it was here, at the age of sixteen, that Patrick was taken captive. Countless able scholars have written, even in recent years, about Patrick's life, character and mission: so many, in fact, that a cynic might be convinced that in the 'seventy-seven' lives of the saint there must be 'seven times seventy-seven' lies. Many of these scholars have vainly sought to locate *Bannavem Taberniae*, weaving all sorts of elaborate theories in the process. Some have attempted to identify the *vicus* with Boulogne, in north-eastern France. Others have opted for Kilpatrick near Dumbarton in Scotland, an identification little favoured in this century because the area was outside the Roman empire. But most situate Calpornius's estate in Roman Britain, south of Hadrian's Wall and on or near the western seaboard within the likely range of Irish raiders. Hence, a *vicus* known as *Bannaventa* (now called Whilton Lodge, near Daventry in Northamptonshire) on the great Roman road of Watling Street, can be ruled out, as a site in central England would have been inaccessible to Irish pirates. Muirchú, in his celebrated *Life*, states that the place in question was Ventre, formerly *Venta Silurum* and now Caerwent, Gwent, south Wales. *Venta Silurum*, however, was an important regional capital or *civitas* and not a mere *vicus*. Glastonbury in Somersetshire, some thirteen miles from the Bristol Channel, has found at least one advocate. So, too, has Tafarn, on the prosperous island of Anglesea (*Manavia* in Roman times), off the north-west coast of Wales. A place formerly called *Banna*, near Birdoswald, on Hadrian's Wall, has also been suggested. Ravenglass, the Romano-British *Clannaventa*, on the coast of Cumberland has some supporters. To the Romans, the Lake District, in which Ravenglass is situated, was strategically important because of its proximity to Hadrian's Wall. Their major work in the area was the road from Ambleside on the shores of Windermere to the coast at Ravenglass, with a fort at either end and a great camp built midway along the route at Hardknott. The original fort at Ravenglass would have developed into a minor administrative unit or *vicus*. A *vicus* on the northern extremities of the Roman empire would certainly help to explain Patrick's poor Latin. There is an obvious etymological objection to this identification because it depends on a supposed scribal error, a mistaken rendering, *Bannaventa*, of the placename *Clannaventa*. Dangerous grounds on which to build a theory!

The attempts to locate *Bannavem Taberniae* have been painstaking but futile to date. No certainty about the identity of this place has been reached nor can be reached until definitive evidence is discovered. All we can say is that the place of Patrick's capture was probably on the west coast of Roman Britain in a region subject to incursions from Ireland and that Patrick's dual background (the fact that he was both a member of the Celto-Roman gentry and also a deacon's son) was very important to him. Loyal to the Church, he was nevertheless fiercely proud of his imperial roots. In fact, as Bieler [1967] points out, 'Roman' and 'Christian' were for Patrick almost synonymous terms.

If the place at which Patrick was captured is unidentifiable, the year of his birth is almost unknowable. Traditionally, it is held that Patrick was born about 385 but many scholars question this date: a few arguing for an earlier date and a number proposing a birth-date in the second decade of the fifth century. Mario Esposito [1958], for instance, believes that Patrick 'lived about 350-430.' Thomas F O'Rahilly and James Carney are of the opinion that the saint was at his most active between 457, or a few years later, and 492/493, with Carney confidently holding that Patrick was born in 422 and died on Wednesday, 17th March 493! It is to be regretted that Carney's certitude did not extend to an exact date for our saint's birth. Irishmen, the world over, might also have celebrated the patron's birthday!

All scholars, then, place the saint's significant years in the fifth century: but one group has him dying when another sees him as in his prime and yet another believes him to have been then just a 'whining schoolboy' creeping snail-like and unwillingly to the local *ludus*. For a quarter of a century, in fact from the time when O'Rahilly gave his controversial lecture during the Second World War until

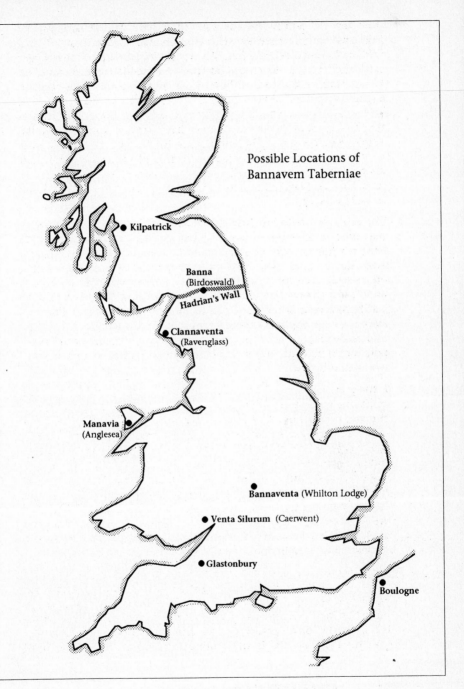

Possible Locations of
Bannavem Taberniae

● Kilpatrick

Banna
(Birdoswald)
Hadrian's Wall

● Clannaventa
(Ravenglass)

Manavia ●
(Anglesea)

● Bannaventa (Whilton Lodge)

● Venta Silurum (Caerwent)

● Glastonbury

● Boulogne

15

Hanson wrote in 1968, the advocates of a totally fifth-century career for Patrick captured most of the attention and made most of the play. Notwithstanding all that, in the last two decades the traditionalists have staged a comeback. The conservative dating of about 432-461 for Patrick's mission, and a birth-date c 385, is now, once more, generally accepted.

This 'orthodox' position has been convincingly bolstered by the contributions of two modern authorities: the Dutch Latinist, Christine Mohrmann, and the Anglican academic and bishop, the late R P C Hanson. Mohrmann made a searching study of Patrick's Latin and came to the conclusion that 'the linguistic facts confirm the general course of events as it is recorded by tradition.' Hanson [1968 and 1983] pieced together a number of fragments of evidence, the cumulative effect of which convinced him that Patrick was born towards the end of the fourth century: Patrick began his truncated schooling before the break-down of the Roman education system in Britain; the most likely time when Calpornius could have been both a deacon and a decurion in fourth-century Britain was between 395 and 399; Patrick's pessimistic fixation with the imminent end of the world is characteristic of the attitude of someone who had lived through the collapse of the Roman empire of which he had felt very much a part; his familiarity with the gold coin, the *solidus*, long out of currency by the second-half of the fifth century, points to a birth-date towards the end of the 300s; the aged Patrick's expressed wish to go 'as far as Gaul, to visit the brethren and to see the face of the saints' [*Confessio* 43] implies a period of peace there, probably between 430 and 460; and, finally, the fact that the British Church sponsored a foreign missionary also suggests a Patrician ministry in Ireland in the first half of the fifth century prior to the turmoil associated with the dissolution of the Roman empire which would have preoccupied that Church at home. The weight of the evidence has been tipped in favour of the traditional dating of our subject and we are happy to place Patrick's birth in the middle years of the last quarter of the fourth century.

Patrick spent six years as a slave in Ireland. He tells us that he was a herdsman and, if Muirchú is to be believed and correctly interpreted, it seems that his enemies dismissively referred to him as the 'Pigman' [Preface i]. Already we have shown how little we know with certainty about the saint. We have been unable to identify the place of his capture. We have had to admit grave doubts regarding the approximate date of his birth. Now, as we begin a discussion of the location of Patrick's place of captivity in Ireland, once more we have to acknowledge that our findings cannot be conclusive.

In his own writings, Patrick mentions only one Irish placename, the controversial *Silva Focluti*. In his account of his vision in which he was invited by Victor to return to the land of his captivity, Patrick mentions the people 'who were near the wood of Voclut which is close to the Western Sea' [*Confessio* 23]. In the late seventh or early eighth century, Tírechán, who compiled an account of Patrick's activities in Ireland, identified this place with 'the wood of Fochloth' in Connaught, a name commonly believed to survive in modern Faughill, near Killala, Co Mayo. The author of the *Brief Account* was himself, of course, a native of this district! The saint's seemingly intimate allusion to this place has been taken by many as a reference to the scene of his captivity and several authorities, Bury, O'Rahilly and Hanson [1983], for example, are convinced that Patrick spent his time as a slave in the west of Ireland.

To make this identification it is necessary for them to dismiss the time-honoured tradition linking the saint with Slemish in Co Antrim as being without foundation and (for some of them) part of the so-called 'Armagh legend'. They have to dismiss altogether the credible theory that the saint's history is in some way tied up with the destiny of the Ulaid, one-time rulers of much of Ulster before being confined to what are now Counties Antrim and Down by the ambitious and advancing Uí Néill. Other scholars refuse to abandon Patrick's supposed links with the north-east and (since in the ancient world the Irish Sea was referred to as the *Mare Occidentale*, the Western Sea, and because of similarities in the Irish forms of the names) associate him with Magherafelt, Co Derry [John Mc Erlean], Killultagh in south Antrim [Eoin Mac Neill; 1923], Kilclief on Strangford Lough, Co Down [Helena Concannon] or Faughal near Cushendall, Co Antrim [Henry Morris]; each advocate proposing that the place he or she favours is the mysterious *Silva Focluti*. Patrick himself speaks of spending much of his servitude 'on the mountains' [*Confessio* 16] in prayer. Slemish, rising to a height of four hundred and thirty-eight metres above sea level, is consistent with the saint's reference to a mountainous district. This is in sharp contrast to the forest plains in the neighbourhood of Killala which can barely even claim to be hilly.

While a northern location for *Silva Focluti* is distinctly possible, a solution to the problem can be arrived at without rejecting the traditional location of *Silva Focluti* in the west of Ireland or the Slemish tradition of the saint's captivity. Patrick may have been in both areas, either because he was sold by a master in one area to a new owner in the other or because, after his six years of captivity in Co Antrim, he escaped to Britain or the continent through a port in Co Mayo.

Such an escape would, admittedly, have been unlikely but would not have been impossible. The discovery of an oil-jar, dredged up a hundred and fifty miles off the west coast, possibly proves that continental merchants came by sea at that time to ports on Ireland's Atlantic coast. In the Brendan voyage, during the summer of 1976, in these very waters, Tim Severin and his crew proved the reliability and efficiency of the ancient Irish curragh; something which sea-going westerners have known, indeed, for generations. But the most acceptable solution to the problem of the location of *Silva Focluti* would seem to be that Patrick knew of its existence in the far west of Ireland but had never been there (just as a man who is 'sent to Coventry' does not automatically find himself in the English midlands) and viewed this remote spot in Co Mayo as a symbol of the furthermost outpost on earth – the equivalent of what the classical writers called *Ultima Thule* – and it was to 'the most remote places, beyond which no man dwells' [*Confessio* 51; see also 34] that Patrick, the missionary, was ultimately to direct his steps.

Before his return to Ireland Patrick had to prepare himself for his mission. Muirchú in his *Life* and Tírechán in his *Brief Account* tell us that the saint spent a considerable time on the continent and received there a belated education. These later hagiographical works are undoubtedly of suspect reliability and Bieler's [1967] advice that 'their evidence must be received with the greatest caution' is salutary. Nevertheless they are essential reading for anyone intent on examining Patrick's theological and spiritual formation.

Muirchú claims that, after some seven years 'in his own country with his relatives' [I,4], Patrick 'set out to visit and honour the apostolic see, the head, that is, of all the churches in the whole world' [I, 5ii]. 'So,' the account proceeds, 'he crossed the sea to the south of Britain and began to travel through Gaul ... But on his way he found a very holy man of approved faith and doctrine, bishop of the city of Auxerre, leader of almost all Gaul, the great lord Germanus' [I,6i]. Muirchú claims that his hero spent thirty or even forty years at the feet of Germanus.

Having thus prepared himself for 'the work of the Gospel' [I,8i], Patrick set out for Ireland, with the priest Segitius as a companion, apparently to assist Palladius. Early in their journey westwards, while the travellers were at *Ebmoria* (which may be Avrolles, less than twenty miles north-east of Auxerre), they were informed of the first bishop's untimely death and Patrick 'had the episcopal grade conferred on him by the holy bishop Amathorex' [I,9i]. (Amator, who died in 418, was Germanus's predecessor at Auxerre and it could be that Muirchú's *Amathorex* refers to him. Perhaps the author of the *Vita* is suggesting that Patrick was consecrated by Germanus, bishop of Auxerre, who is spoken of in the same way as we might refer to the present Pope as 'Peter'? It may be that Muirchú confuses Patrick's consecration as a bishop by Germanus, which he alludes to elsewhere, with his earlier ordination to the priesthood or diaconate by Amator.) On the same day, Muirchú's record states, 'Auxilius, Iserninus and others were ordained to lower grades' [I,9 (iii)]. The party then made its way 'speedily' to Ireland.

Tírechán has Patrick spend 'seven years' travelling 'on water, in plains, and in mountain valleys throughout Gaul and the whole of Italy and the islands in the Tyrrhene Sea' [III,1 (vi)]. The Connachtman quotes Bishop Ultán as the source of his information that Patrick stayed for thirty years 'in one of these islands, which is called Aralanensis' (which some writers have, wrongly, it seems, identified as Lérins). Buried elsewhere [II,4 (i-iv)] in Tírechán's *Brief Account* are the three so-called *Sayings of Patrick*. The first of these *Sayings* (perhaps from what the author refers to as Patrick's 'account of his labours') is the statement: 'I had the fear of God as my guide through Gaul and Italy and the islands in the Tyrrhene Sea' [II 4i]. The authenticity of this *Saying of Patrick*, eighteen words of Latin in all, a single sentence, is of crucial importance for we may have here evidence from the saint's own pen or tongue which confirms Patrick's continental training while making no exaggerated claims regarding its duration.

Bieler [1967] believes that this *Saying* 'might well be genuine, though the possibility that it is spurious cannot be categorically excluded'. He feels that, 'Its language might well be Patrick's.' The Austrian scholar then goes on to suggest that the saint trained under Saint Germanus at his island monastery (which he is satisfied is Tírechán's elusive *Aralanensis*) in the river Yonne at Auxerre, may have visited shrines, like Tours, in Gaul and Italy and may have called at primitive monastic foundations on islands in the Tyrrhene Sea and possibly at Lérins, just off the modern resort of Cannes. The Cistercian monks who currently occupy the isle of Saint-Honorat, in the islands of Lérins, proudly boast of its Patrician associations. The very ancient Church of the Blessed Trinity on the island, which dates back to the time of the monastery's foundation by Honoratus (d 430), is trefoil in shape and structure and so it may not be too whimsical of us to speculate that a visit to this chapel might have inspired Patrick to use the shamrock in his supposed famous demonstration of the mystery of the Trinity. Bieler believes that 'the general impression' which one gets from Patrick's Latin is that 'it is continental' and that 'linguistic evidence does not go very far in supporting the theory that Patrick's Latin is British.' The palaeographer and Late Latinist is supported in this by the acute scholarship of Professor Christine Mohrmann. Two recent writers on Patrick's career, Bishop Joseph Duffy and the late Doctor John Morris, are convinced of the basic validity of Bieler's approach. In his essay, *Ex Saliva Scripturae Mea*, David Howlett argues that the saint was actually a competent exegete. He would, then, have been the product of a sophisticated scriptural school, presumably on the continent rather than in more backward Britain. This essay [1989] has not yet, of course, been subjected to the scrutiny of experts.

Bishop Hanson [1968] feels that Patrick is 'wholly the product of the British Church', that his mission was sponsored (and indeed also impeded) by British churchmen, that his language typifies the Vulgar Latin of fifth-century Britain and that the saint was not influenced to any appreciable extent by a continental training, though 'he probably did pay a visit to Gaul.' Above all, Hanson dismisses the attribution of the key *Saying* to Patrick, claiming that it does 'not recall either Patrick's style or vocabulary' and placing it in 'a later age than his, perhaps the seventh century or later.' While Hanson handsomely acknowledges Ludwig Bieler's unique contribution to Patrician studies, it is to be regretted that he does not attempt, in his second book on this particular subject, *The Life and Writings of the Historical Saint Patrick* (New York, 1983), to demolish the case for a continental training for the apostle of Ireland made by Bieler in his *Saint Patrick and the Coming of Christianity* (Dublin, 1967). Hanson laments the fact that Professor Mohrmann 'had apparently not read' Kenneth Jackson's most pertinent book on *Language and History in Early Britain* (Edinburgh, 1953): otherwise she would have been persuaded of the validity of the bishop's position. Clearly Doctor Bieler's education was not similarly defective for he uses Jackson's insights to reach a diametrically opposite conclusion to Hanson's! It must be obvious that while the specialists differ no definite conclusions in this particular area can be reached.

Happily, scholarly consensus is not required for an appreciation of Patrick's character and mind. He is to be met in his own writings. The *Sayings* provide us with no useful information in this regard. They are short in the extreme. We do not have to consider them in our present discussion. We can also ignore the *First Synod of Saint Patrick*. Whether it is authentic or not is unimportant at this juncture since the work deals with sober ecclesiastical legislation and can tell nothing about our subject (save, perhaps, to throw some light on his attitude to church laws and structures). We are left, then, with the two documents which the saint seems definitely to have composed and which contain a wealth of information about Patrick. Primarily a powerful, corrective appeal to deviant Christians, the *Epistola* is impregnated with clues about Patrick's personality and outlook. It is in the halting language of the *Confessio* in particular, however, that Patrick comes alive to us. The *Confessio* may be a most frustrating book to read. It is, indeed, poorly written, in ungrammatical Late Latin by a man who had no mastery of the language and yet, because of these very limitations, it is an amazingly honest and revealing document, of crucial importance for anyone who wants to understand the man and his mind.

What picture emerges from his own writings of Patrick? Undoubtedly one of a very real, admirable and lovable human being, most striking perhaps in his humility. It was customary for authors in the fifth century to begin with wordy declarations of inadequacy and Patrick follows this convention in both his works. But his is not the feigned humility of an early Uriah Heep, 'the 'umblest person going'. Patrick has a genuine sense of his unworthiness and inferiority, as compared with others or with the ideal of the divine law. He is without arrogance. Although a bishop and a leader of the Irish Christians, he can still see himself as a stone that had been lifted up out of the mud. He has no intellectual pretensions and recognises the enormous gaps in his education and his inability to express himself on paper. He sorrowfully but readily admits his sinfulness. Recognition of his own limitations does not, however, render him impotent or even force him to curb his tongue. When the occasion demands it, he can be fiercely assertive, castigating Coroticus and his minions for their crimes and defending himself vigorously against malicious allegations. A stranger to Ireland and unprotected by its social structure, he can nevertheless dynamically pursue and achieve his missionary aims.

Patrick displays great independence of mind and tenacity. No difficulty seems to daunt him. Physically strong and a man of enormous energy and great courage, he is determined and resolute. His self-confessed inadequate formal education is only a partial disability for he has the practical man's gift of getting his message across. Patrick would appear to have been a most highly organised and successful administrator. As Hanson [1968] observes, he involves himself with humdrum financial management, doubtless one of the more irksome chores of the episcopacy. He carries out the onerous sacramental and religious functions of a bishop with zeal and alacrity: baptising, confirming, ordaining, celebrating the Eucharist and inducting monks and nuns. He finds time to oversee the education of clerical students.

In spite of his imperfections as an author, he is, too, an excellent communicator, a born orator and a first-rate public relations man.

He is prudent and patient and has not the impetuousity that often accompanies decisiveness. He does not take unneccessary risks nor rush headlong into traps but rather takes precautions and pays protection-money to those who can affect his future [Confessio 52]. His is the long-term view regarding the ultimate success of his mission and thence he avoids any reason for being accused of simony and resolves never to abandon his infant Church by returning, even on holiday, to Britain. He is also resilient. While life has dealt him many blows, he does not give in to disillusionment or despair. Nor has adversity managed to stifle his sense of humour. He can still manage the occasional tongue-in-cheek aside [Confessio 13 and 49, for instance].

Neither does Patrick have the ruthlessness that sometimes diminishes the man of action. He has faults, of course: he is racist in his attitude to the Picts; he is snobbish and rather smug when 'one particular blessed Irish maiden, nobly-born and very beautiful' [Confessio 42] accepts baptism from him and resolves to devote herself to the religious life; he is obsessed by the deficiencies in his education. But he is a person of great warmth, compassion and sympathy. He feels keenly for the wretched victims of the horrible slave system. He is sympathetic to the plight of the weak and suffering. He is capable of friendship (so that he can bitterly regret betrayal and the reduction in stature that this has brought about in his 'very dear friend' [Confessio 32]). He is loathe to hurt others even when necessary and is uninterested in his own material well-being. The saint's kindliness and generosity make him attractive to all he meets: but especially to women and the young. As Helena Concannon recognised almost sixty years ago, Patrick views 'women as active workers in the missionary field.' But it is more than this: he is profoundly and sensitively open to women and, as Noel Dermot O'Donoghue perceives, 'has in himself a certain vulnerability, which nevertheless does not take refuge in a grim and pretentious asceticism, nor yet in that neurotic fear and contempt for the feminine which has entered so deeply into the attitudes and structures of the Christian Church in its main manifestations. In this sense he is a complete man.' He is also able to make a powerful appeal to the generosity of young people so that the sons of kings travel around with him and 'the sons of the Irish and the daughters of local kings have become monks and are virgins dedicated to Christ' [Confessio 41].

Through all this we never lose sight of his fragile, human nature. Indeed, perhaps it is, honestly presented, his greatest charism. Over and over again in his writings, we can see that even as an old man he is still attempting to cope with the loneliness and hurts suffered by the cosseted adolescent who had been dragged into slavery in an alien land. To the end of his days he sees himself as a slave and an exile, isolated and unwanted. His vulnerability is also shown by the facts that years later he can still smart at the memory of the treachery of a friend, can still long for the warmth of home and can still writhe from the cruelty of unjustified criticism. To have been torn from his congenial background and to have been dragged off into slavery in an alien and pagan environment must have been a frightful and, indeed, traumatic experience for a boy who up until then had been a carefree adolescent. And Patrick's writings give us ample evidence that he was so traumatised.

Patrick had within him, perhaps, the seeds of self-destruction. He was dynamic and magnetic and yet pathetic and vulnerable. He might have been paralysed by the conflicting sides to his character but he managed to cope with his difficult personality and, in fact, to make himself into a most interesting and significant figure in history. The reason for this double success, in self-acceptance and in his contribution to mankind, was undoubtedly the intensity of his faith in and relationship with God. He was a prayerful person with a burning love for Christ whom he regarded as his one, true friend, forever bolstering, encouraging and protecting him. Out of this continuing encounter with Christ grew his urgent evangelism, his genuine charity which disposed him to love those who persecuted and scorned him, his ardent desire for martyrdom, his delighted anticipation of the imminent Second Coming, and his trusting acceptance of God's providential ordering of his life.

Almost continuous daily prayer, regular reception of or contact with the sacraments, frequent interventions by the Holy Spirit in dreams or visions, and a lifelong openness to the word of God through the Bible allowed Patrick to become God's vessel and simultaneously to realise his full human potential. Helena Concannon observes, 'It was because Patrick was a great saint that he was a great missioner.' Doubtless Patrick recognised this, for his writings, and particularly the *Confessio*, are a triumphal, grateful and sincere statement of thanks to Almighty God. While it is most definitely not the saint's own composition, the hymn attributed to him really says it all:

Christ with me, Christ before me,
Christ behind me, Christ within me,
Christ beneath me, Christ above me,

Christ at my right hand, Christ at my left,
Christ in front,
Christ in the chariot-seat,
Christ in the poop.
Christ in the heart of every man who thinks of me,
Christ in the mouth of every man who speaks to me,
Christ in every eye that sees me,
Christ in every ear that hears me. Amen.

Notes:

1. Numerous translations of the authentic Patrician texts have been produced within the last one hundred years. The translations of Wright, Healy and White, now out of copyright, are readable but rather dated. Since these versions have been superseded by the editions of scholars like Conneely, De Paor, Duffy, Hanson and Hood, the earnest reader is advised to consult the modern authoritative works.

2. The three *Dicta Patricii* are to be found in Tírechán's *Brief Account* [II,4] and can be translated as follows:

(i)

I had the fear of God as my guide through Gaul and Italy and the islands in the Tyrrhene Sea.

(ii)

You have gone from this world to paradise. Thanks be to God.

(iii)

Church of the Irish, or rather of the Romans! In order that you may be Christians like the Romans, you must chant in your churches at every hour of prayer that commendable utterance: 'Kyrie Eleison, Christe Eleison'. Let every church which follows me sing, 'Kyrie Eleison, Christe Eleison'. Thanks be to God.

CHAPTER THREE

Patrick: The Mission and its Setting

'... when Patrick came
the worship of idols was abolished
and the Catholic faith spread
over our whole country.'

[Muirchú]

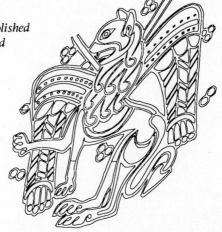

T he social, political and religious climate into which Patrick's mission brought him, in 432 or thereabouts, was different from anything he may have experienced in Britain. It was not something with which he was totally unfamiliar, however, for he was himself a Celt, albeit a Briton, and his six years of servitude in Ireland had prepared him, to some extent at least, for the culture with which he was going to have to deal.

The Ireland of Patrick's time was an agglomeration of numerous, independent small kingdoms, all agrarian but at various stages of development, linked by proximity and by a shared tongue. There were perhaps about one hundred and fifty of these *tuatha* in fifth-century Ireland, each ruled by a king. The *tuath* (the word means 'a people') was the basic political entity in early Ireland. Any group of people, large enough to be ruled by a king and conscious of its distinct identity, could regard itself as a *tuath*. We have no precise idea how any particular *tuath* perceived itself territorially but can say that, since wealth was measured in agricultural produce, it must have been linked inextricably to exclusive possession of a significantly large tract of land. *Tuatha* joined together in loose federations to form more powerful local kingdoms, dominated by greater over-kings. These alliances were personal agreements (guaranteed by the giving of hostages to the over-king and by the acceptance of a stipend from him) between individual inferior kings and a stronger king. The king of a single *tuath* still had the absolute allegiance of his own people. And groups of these confederations of local kingdoms allied themselves with one another to make up provincial kingdoms, controlled by superior, provincial kings. There was no such personage in Ancient Ireland as a 'High King', sovereign of the entire island.

In the north of Ireland one of the great kingdoms was that of the Ulaid. Originally they would appear to have held sway in somewhat more than what is to-day the nine-county province of Ulster. Their capital was at *Emhain Macha*, the great pagan holy place, close to the modern city of Armagh. They were gradually overshadowed and pushed eastwards, probably in the middle years of the fifth century, by the northern Uí Néill, reputedly descended from Niall Noígiallach. The northern Uí Néill would seem to have encouraged and supported the creation and continued existence of a string of satellite kingdoms. These were known as the *Airgialla* ('the hostage givers') and were a sort of buffer-state between the Uí Néill and the Ulaid in what is mid-Ulster.

Around the same time, another group, the southern Uí Néill displaced the Laigin, the original inhabitants of Leinster, and set up a confederation of kingdoms in Meath, Westmeath, Longford, and parts of Louth, Dublin and Offaly. These Uí Néill, relatives of the self-designated descendants of Niall Noígiallach, were a branch of the Connachta, rulers of a great provincial kingdom in the west of Ireland. The south-east of the island continued to be the preserve of the Laigin who had constantly to defend themselves from the pressure of their northern neighbours. In *Mumu* or Munster the most powerful kings were the Eoganachta, a dynasty whose main settlement was at Cashel.

The king of a simple *tuath* was the weakest type of king, and as a result would have found it convenient to enter into a relationship with one more powerful than he. The Irish king was called a *rí*: a word obviously related to the Gaulish *rix* and the Latin *rex*. In his own kingdom his powers were limited and he had very little controlling authority. He was not a judge over his people, for instance; nor could he enact laws. But he did lead the people in time of war, was their representative in peacetime, presided over the annual assembly (the *óenach*) of his people, and originally, at least, would seem to have been afforded some sort of sacerdotal dignity.

The sacred character of the king is demonstrated by the taboos and

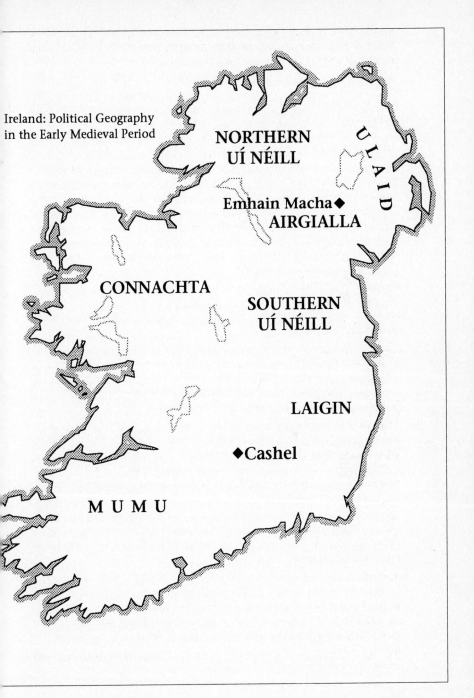

Ireland: Political Geography
in the Early Medieval Period

NORTHERN
UÍ NÉILL

ULAID

Emhain Macha◆
AIRGIALLA

CONNACHTA

SOUTHERN
UÍ NÉILL

LAIGIN

◆Cashel

M U M U

prerogatives which were attached to him and by the fact that he had always to be accompanied by an appropriate retinue and could never use implements considered degrading.

A king was seen as being somehow married to his *tuath* and the inauguration ceremonies of kings, even apparently as late as the twelfth century when Giraldus Cambrensis wrote his *Topographia Hiberniae* (*Topography of Ireland*), would appear to have involved some sort of primitive mating rites. The word *feis* is used to describe a king's inauguration. *Feis* is usually translated as 'feast' but the word actually has its root in the Archaic Old Irish verb 'to spend the night with or to sleep with or to marry'. Each *tuath* had its own proper site for 'proclaiming' its king and specified representatives of subordinate friendly families to perform particular ceremonies on the occasion. The kings of the northern Uí Néill, for instance, had their inauguration site at Tullaghogue, near Cookstown, and the Uí Catháin (O'Kane) and the Uí hAgáin (O'Hagan) were essential partners in the legal installation of the Uí Néill.

Next to the king in Irish society ranked the land-owning nobles. And on a level with this group were the learned class, the *áes dána*, a unique group with special privileges. This class contained the *filid* or poets and the druids who were respected for their skill, learning and magic. Members of the *áes dána* were protected by law even outside their own *tuath* and so operated locally but received some sort of national recognition. Below them were the freemen and the small farmers. The lowest class of all were the unfree: slaves, labourers, workmen, mercenaries and simple entertainers.

One of the most important aspects of this society was a person's status and honour. A king's status was dependent upon the number of *tuatha* subordinate to him, a noble's on the number of his clients or vassals and a commoner's simply on the extent of his possessions. Honour was measured in terms of units of cattle. A king had a higher honour price than a noble who, in turn, had a greater honour price than a mere freeman. A man's honour price determined the limits of what he could legally do. Honour, status and clientship were the basis of Irish law, giving everyone his fixed place in a pyramidical Irish society.

Early Irish civilisation laid great stress on family relationships. The significant family group was not the modern 'nuclear family' (parents and children) but the kin-group or *derbhfhine* which was made up of all those males who were descended from a common great-grandfather. This society was dominated by men. A woman had the status of her husband or nearest male relative. The *derbhfhine* acted as a body and members had responsibility, in varying degrees, for the actions of other family members. Membership of a ruling *derbhfhine* made a man eligible for election to the kingship of his *tuath*, provided he was both physically and morally unblemished. This system produced credible candidates for the office but often provoked rivalry and conflict.

The early Irish dwelt in ring-forts, crannogs and unenclosed houses. Ring-forts are very numerous and are to be found in all parts of the country. Some authorities suggest that there were up to forty thousand forts in the island. There are several words in the Irish language for 'fort' and these, or anglicised versions of them, often form part of the names of our townlands: *lios, ráth, cathair, caiseal* and *dún*. The first two refer to earthen structures; the second two words describe stone constructions; and the final word is normally used to designate a particularly large fort.

The rath is the most common. Simply stated, it may be described as a circular open space surrounded by a bank or fosse and a palisade. The diameter of the enclosed space can be as small as fifteen metres or as much as sixty metres. Some Irish raths date from as early as 1000BC but the large majority seem to belong to the early Christian period; that is, from the fifth to the tenth centuries. In Ulster, archaeologists have found occupation material datable to the period between the twelfth and the sixteenth centuries. Nevertheless, it is generally held that, while some forts continued in use until the Plantation, the construction of raths did not persist beyond the Middle Ages. The rath seems to have been a simple farmstead, the ring-fort enclosing houses and farm buildings and affording some protection (from wolves, for example) to our primitive farmers. Fifth-century Ireland was a totally agrarian society. In fact, there were no towns in the island until the arrival of the Vikings. Timber, stone, clay, turf and wattle-and-daub were employed in the construction of the buildings inside raths.

Crannogs are man-made islands in lakes or bogs on which our primitive ancestors erected dwellings. These artificial islands were constructed of logs (hence the word *crannog* which comes from the Irish word for a tree), turf, stones, brushwood and animal bones. A crannog was occupied by one single nuclear family and its servants. Crannogs are much less numerous than ring-forts. There is some archaeological evidence for prehistoric occupation of crannogs but the majority belong, like the ring-forts, to the early Christian period. The less prosperous Irish of this time would have lived in unenclosed, timber and clay houses, examples of which have been found especially in Munster.

The one feature of his adopted environment that must have particularly disturbed Patrick was Celtic religion. We have a very incomplete knowledge of Celtic paganism in Ireland. Information about it comes from three sources: classical allusions to Celtic religious practices especially in Gaul; the names of divinities preserved in inscriptions and placenames; and the oldest strata of Irish and Welsh heroic literature. Irish paganism presumably bore a close similarity to the Celtic religion of Britain and particularly Gaul, which is much better known.

The Irish Celts, like their continental cousins, had sanctuaries associated with rivers, springs and wells. Water everywhere has been seen as life-giving. The waters of baptism, for instance, are rich in symbolism for Christians. Rivers and wells have been associated with fertility and motherhood and also with strength, destruction and purification. Just as in France the rivers Marne and Seine (the *Matrona* and the *Sequana*) were sacred to certain goddesses, so the Boyne and the Shannon were linked to the goddesses *Boand* and *Sinann*. It seems that the sacred rites at *Samhain* (1st November), the great Celtic New Year festival, of which our Hallowe'en is a survival, were held on the banks of rivers or on the shores of lakes. It is probably no accident either that Irish Catholics show such devotion to the Church's great annual commemoration of the dead at this particular time of year. Wells, too, would appear to have been the *foci* of ritual practice. The well was thought of as one of the entrances to the otherworld. Even in the twentieth century, holy wells, often still situated beside the ancient ecclesiastical foundations which gave them Christian respectability, have cultic associations.

The Irish, like the continental Celts, venerated certain trees and groves of trees. The oak was particularly sacred. The Celts commonly applied the term *nemeton* to sacred groves. Drunemeton in Galicia in Spain was one such sanctuary. *Nemeton* is related to the Latin *nemus*, 'a grove', and is the root of the Irish word *neimheadh*, 'a sanctuary'. As Christianity replaced paganism in Ireland, shrines in oak-groves were adopted by the new religionists and adapted to their own purposes. Other sacred trees in Celtic Ireland were the hazel, the rowan and the yew. Many of our present towns and townlands enshrine the names of these trees. For instance, the yew survives in Newry ('the yew tree of the head of the strand') and Altinure ('the cliff of the yew tree'). Even unspecified trees are recorded in some of our placenames: Moville, for example, means simply 'the plain of the tree'. It is easy to see why trees should have been considered sacred: trees unite the heavens, the earth and the underworld; they can be tall and stately; they are not inanimate but living and so could be seen as being possessed by a god or a spirit; leafless in winter but covered in foliage in summer, they represent fertility and rebirth; they have a certain indestructibility and resistance to the elements of fire and water. It would seem that trees were sometimes a focal point in a sanctuary. This reverence for trees was continued into the Christian era. Kildare, the 'church of the oak', is a good example. They were often also linked to venerated wells (in the case of Derry, the 'oak-grove', with what is now known as Saint Columb's Well).

Burial and sacrifice, with their associations with death and the after-life, had religious implications even for pagans. Burial mounds inevitably were Celtic holy places. It seems that the Celts had a cult of graves and that they may have taken over the cairns and other burial places of earlier peoples, the great tumuli of Newgrange, Knowth and Dowth in the Boyne Valley and Emhain Macha, for instance. These sites would seem to have been considered as entrances to the otherworld and as the dwelling-places of divine ancestors.

A consideration of the sanctuaries of the pagan Irish Celts inevitably leads on to further mention of the pagan priests who officiated at these shrines. Our information on this subject comes from classical authors like Caesar, who had some knowledge of the situation in Gaul but who knew nothing about conditions in Ireland. The druids were recruited from the warrior aristocracy and taught the continuity of life beyond the grave. Just as the modern fundamentalist Imam inspires the Muslim soldier to bravery with the promise of eternal life, so the druid encouraged warriors to hold their own lives in small regard. The druids were engaged in the practice of magic, divination and ritual and in the offering of sacrifice, sometimes human sacrifice, to the gods. Indeed, when these skilled practitioners in magic are mentioned in early texts in Latin of an Irish provenance, they are referred to as *magi*. They were also judges as well as priests. Accordingly, they would have led religious ceremonies, settled legal disputes, and served as advisers to their people.

The human head is the most typical Celtic religious symbol of divinity and the otherworld. The Celts were head-hunters and, like other head-hunting warriors, considered severed heads as war-trophies, but they went much further. They venerated the head, imbuing it with all the qualities and powers most admired and most desired by them – fertility, prophecy, hospitality, wisdom and healing. The Iron Age three-faced figures from Corleck, Co Cavan and from Woodlands, Raphoe, Co Donegal; the janiform heads at Boa Island, Co Fermanagh and at Kilnaboy, Co Clare; the numerous stone heads to be seen in our museums – all testify to the importance of the head in the religious lives of the pagan Celts.

The Irish Celts worshipped a horned god. There are several carvings which survive giving iconographic evidence for this cult in Ireland: a figure now housed in the chapter-house of the Church of Ireland Cathedral in Armagh; one of the stones on Boa Island; the head from Cortynan, Co Armagh; and Christian portrayals of a horned deity, possibly symbolic of Satan, on the Market Cross at Kells, the north pillar at Clonmacnois, and the stele at Carndonagh, Co Donegal. These give convincing testimony to the presence in Ireland of veneration of a god similar to the stag-god Cernunnos worshipped by the Celts in Gaul.

Cernunnos was sometimes equated with Mercury, Mars or Jupiter and is linked with wealth and prosperity, warfare, fecundity and virility. One of his emblems is the serpent, universally recognised as a phallic symbol. It is probably no coincidence that the medieval carving (see page 49) of Saint Patrick from Faughart, Co Louth, now in the National Museum of Ireland, has the saint trampling on a serpent. Of all the Celtic deities, the horned god Cernunnos, with his associations with fertility, would have been anathema to Christians. Patrick tells us that, up until his arrival in the country, the Irish had worshipped 'idols and things impure' [*Confessio* 41]. He may have been referring vaguely to fertility rites and the use of male or female (the sheela-na-gig) fertility symbols or he may be speaking especially of the pernicious cult of Cernunnos (or whatever the Irish called this particular member of their Pantheon). Patrick's supposed banishment of all the serpents from Ireland may be a vivid and subtle way of recalling how he destroyed pagan devotion to the horned god and his attendant serpents.

The Celts had a warrior god whose influence was confined not merely to warfare but who was the tribal god, the father and protector of his people. He was known by different names and for different attributes in various parts of Ireland: *An Dagda, Lugh Lámhfhada, Da Choc, Tuathal, Segomo, Nuadu* and *Cumhal*. They also had supposedly powerful female deities: the national goddesses *Eriu, Banba* and *Fótla*; divinities linked with specific places like *Aíne, Grian* and *Macha*; *Anu* and *Danu*, the mothers of certain Irish gods; mother goddesses who were interested in the well-being of humans in particular localities; and fertility goddesses like *Brigit*, the supposed daughter of *An Dagda*, whose festival in the Celtic pagan calendar was *Imbolc*, later christianised as the feast of Saint Brigit on 1st February.

Another great pagan festival of the Celts was *Bealtaine* on 1st May. It marked the beginning of the grazing season when cattle were put out to grass. It may be connected with worship of the god *Belenus*, a diety with a far-flung cult in Celtic lands and associated primarily

Carved figure on Boa Island, Co Fermanagh
Photo: courtesy Northern Ireland Tourist Board

with pastoralism. Great fires were lit throughout the island and the druids drove the cattle between lines of flames to protect them against disease. King Loiguire's fire at Tara was perhaps part of the *Bealtaine* rite and not, as Muirchú suggests, a rite of spring which Patrick could oppose with his rival Easter fire.

Saint Patrick refers unfavourably to the Irish practice of sun-worship. Newgrange, the magnificent Stone Age tumulus in the Boyne Valley, was the chief Irish centre for sun-worship. It is, of course, originally pre-Celtic but may have been adopted by Celts for such a cult. From the Bronze Age onwards, the sun god, one of the most important of the Celtic deities, was associated with both light and death. The wheel, from which, perhaps, evolved the 'ring' which features on our great High Crosses, and the swastika were early sun signs.

For the Celts birds were otherworldly agents, emblems of the gods, heralds of death, and portents of good or bad fortune. Certain birds, the swan and the raven, for example, were connected with the Celtic solar cults. The swan was also a symbol of purity, erotic love, music and gentleness. The raven is less benign. Some authorities are of the opinion that the Celtic god Lugh was originally a raven-god. Lugh developed into a multi-purpose deity – warrior, magician, artist and seer. Lugh's feast was the midsummer festival of *Lughnasa*, traces of which have survived in our own Puck and Lammas fairs, our festivities in Munster on Saint John's Eve and the annual Croagh Patrick pilgrimage on 'Reek Sunday' in the west of Ireland {Note 1}. The flight and sound of the raven was used for divination and was of special importance in ominous prognosis. The wren, too, was apparently used in forecasting evil events and impending misfortune: hence, doubtless, its unpopularity in some Irish country districts even today on the morning of Saint Stephen's Day. The crane was also viewed as a sinister messenger. It seems to have been seen as primarily feminine and promiscuous. The Christian Church, at any rate, objected to the use of birds for augury. In the *Lorica* (*Breastplate*) attributed to Colum Cille, the saint is presented as saying, 'I do not adore the voices of birds ... My druid is Christ the Son of God.' The famous concern shown by Adomnan's Columba for the pathetic, storm-driven crane may, we feel, be more than a record of his pre-Franciscan kindness to dumb creatures. Perhaps it is a subtle way of saying that he and his monks had lost their fear of the agents of a pagan world?

Finally, we note that animals as well as birds played a part in the religion of the pagan Celts. It is possible that certain Celtic gods were originally of beast-like form and later were given human features.

The boar, the bull, the stag, the horse, the ram, and the hound all have firm places in Irish mythology.

This is the environment into which Patrick the Briton arrived to convert the people of the furthermost outpost on earth, 'before the end of the world' [*Confessio* 34]. Patrick seems to have regarded those to whom he was preaching as being entirely pagan. He mentions that the Irish, until his arrival, 'worshipped idols and things impure' [*Confessio* 41]. He appears to have been particularly offended by sun-worship for in chapter 60 of the *Confessio* he seems to be condemning specifically those who adored the sun as opposed to 'the true Sun, Christ'.

We cannot doubt that his mission was successful. He tells us himself that he baptised 'many thousands' [*Confessio* 50], a remarkable achievement at a time when the population of the island numbered only about five hundred thousand. And this is the boast of a patently humble individual! As well as baptising and confirming, he was also anxious to build up a native clergy [*Confessio* 38] and to encourage men and women to take up some form of the religious life [*Confessio* 41, 42, 49; *Epistola* 12, 15, 19]. His respectful attitude to the beautiful and aristocratic would-be nun [*Confessio* 43] shows, as Noel Dermot O'Donoghue has pointed out, that he was 'deeply and sensitively open to women and womanhood': an approach which is undoubtedly Christ-like but which was completely alien to the chauvinism of male-dominated, fifth-century Irish society.

We can surmise that Patrick's teaching would have been simple. He shows himself unaware of the theological controversies of his time such as Pelagianism, and his creed is a straightforward statement of the basic tenets of Christianity {Note 2}. Patrick may or may not have used a shamrock as a teaching aid to get across the doctrine of the Blessed Trinity, but his Rule of Faith [*Confessio* 4] suggests that he presented his listeners with an uncomplicated introduction to the mysteries of the Godhead. In a similar fashion he taught them about the divinity and humanity of Christ, and sinful man's dependence on Christ for salvation. He himself had been carried through his slavery in Ireland by a very basic faith. At the same time he had gained a sympathy for and an understanding of the Irish. No other missionary would have been able to preach with such empathy.

Furthermore, Patrick the Briton must have had a deep awareness of the peculiar preoccupation the Celts had with triunities. Miranda Green's very recent publication, *Symbol and Image in Celtic Religious Art* (London, 1990), stresses the particular importance groups of three had for the Celts. They viewed significant parts of the world around them in triplets: the heavens, the earth and the underworld; earth, air and water; past, present and future; and so on. Their society was organised in a tripartite hierarchy of kings, nobles and freemen. The numbers three (3), three squared (9) and three cubed (27) were all regarded by them as sacred. Most significantly, Doctor Green holds that the idea of divinity having a triple identity was a key element in Celtic religion. This is to be seen, above all, in their three-faced stone idols. The Irish, then, were more open than pagan non-Celts to being convinced of the truth of the central Christian belief in the Trinity.

Patrick's six years in Ireland would have given him an awareness of its socio-political structures. He knew that Ireland was made up of numerous independent *tuatha* and was a hierarchical society. To succeed Patrick had to fit Christianity into the society in which he was working. Above all he had to build up a native priesthood, otherwise his work would have failed within a generation. As an outsider, kinless and without status, he had also to seek the protection of the powerful people in each local kingdom. It seems that he often bought the good-will of kings and their legal advisers, the druids. But this did not guarantee him freedom from danger and persecution. He tells us himself that his life was twelve times at risk, that he was often beaten up and that he daily faced the possibility of robbery, renewed slavery or even death. Sometimes his protectors had to negotiate his release when communications broke down or unfriendly forces intervened [*Confessio* 52].

As well as the dangers posed by men, Patrick had to cope with the difficulties presented by Ireland's inhospitable terrain and climate. Assuming that weather-patterns have not changed dramatically in the interim, the country's inclement weather requires no further comment! Fifth-century Ireland was heavily afforested and many regions of the country were practically inaccessible. There was only the most rudimentary network of roads. When Giraldus Cambrensis was writing, seven hundred years later, it took 'eight days at forty miles a day' to get from south Kerry to north-west Donegal and four days to travel from Dublin to 'the sea beyond Connaught'. And the country's infrastructure hardly disimproved in the meantime! Much travel was done by boat.

The island had a sparse and widely scattered population. A lot of Patrick's time, therefore, must have been taken up with getting from one place to another in the parts of the island to which he devoted his attention. As he moved from district to district, he had to overcome the natural distrust of strangers always to be found in closely-knit and isolated societies. He would also have had to conquer the prejudice against the introduction of a new faith. This may have been shown by those who had a vested interest in the existing order of things {Note 3}.

Patrick's policy was one of inculturation: that is, wherever possible he would have attempted to adapt the cherished religious values and practices of the Celts to Christianity. However, he would seem to have made no effort to accommodate certain of their approaches. Oak-groves, sacred wells and some festivals were easily incorporated into the new religion and the new clergy was soon to find a privileged position as part of the *áes dána*, but obnoxious cults like the worship of 'idols and things impure' [*Confessio* 41], sun-worship, the sucking of another's nipples as a bond of friendship and the eating of food offered to false gods, were repugnant to him and he made every effort to stamp them out. Later tradition highlights his conflicts with the druids. He also studiously avoided giving any suggestion of simony, partially financing his mission himself and refusing stipends and even donations [*Confessio* 50]. This unbending adherence to principle was viewed as intransigence by his critics, who were probably also his sponsors, in Britain. Patrick wanted his motives to be viewed as totally pure and unselfinterested.

Patrick's mission involved numerous setbacks, as, for example, the loss of the newly-baptised congregation at the hands of Coroticus and his soldiers, and entailed great personal sacrifice. This is most clearly seen in his difficult but judicious decision never to leave his flock by returning home, tempting though that prospect must have been. But it was an enormously successful mission. This was due in part to his own Celtic background, in part to his familiarity with the country since boyhood, in part to the commonsense approach he adopted to the task in hand, in part to the magnetism and determination of the man, but above all, as he himself was the first gratefully to acknowledge, to the grace and guidance given to him by Almighty God.

Notes:
1. Lugh is commemorated in placenames as widely separated as León in Spain, Lyons and Loudun in France, Leiden in Holland, London in England and our own Louth. The ancient name of Carlisle in Cumberland was *Luguvalium*.

2. Patrick's pastoral theology is discussed in Daniel Conneely, *The Letters of Saint Patrick* (Maynooth,1993).

3. Too much stress should not perhaps be laid on this last point for, as Gearóid Mac Niocaill has observed, Celtic paganism was not aggressively proselytising and the Irish heathens, like the Athenians with their altar 'to an unknown god', doubtless had that tolerance of other gods typical of polytheists.

CHAPTER FOUR

Patrick and the Church of Armagh

*'Great Armagh remains
with a host of venerable heroes....
The name of Patrick, splendid, famous,
this is the one which grows.'*

[Prologue to
*The Martyrology
of Oengus,*c 800]

Muirchú, author of the *Vita Pátricii* (*Life of Patrick*) and Tírechán, compiler of the *Breviarium* (*Brief Account*), both claim to give us important information on Saint Patrick. We propose to discuss these early medieval documents and then to examine what light they, and other relevant sources from the period, including the *Liber Angeli* (*The Book of the Angel*), throw on the significant topic of Patrick's associations with Armagh.

In recent times, three editions of Muirchú have been published. The latest is to be found in Liam de Paor's *Saint Patrick's World* (Blackrock, Co Dublin, 1993). Ludwig Bieler's last contribution to Patrician studies before his death was *The Patrician Texts in the Book of Armagh* (Dublin, 1979). This gives, among other things, his edition of the *Life*. A year earlier, A E B Hood edited and translated the *Vita Patricii* in his *St Patrick: His Writings and Muirchu's Life* (London and Chichester, 1978). For convenience, Bieler's translation will be accepted as definitive {Note 1}.

Muirchú was a priest of the archdiocese of Armagh. He compiled his *Life* at the suggestion of Bishop Aed of Sleibte (Co Laois) who had affiliated his church to the *paruchia Patricii* (the confederation of Patrician churches) between 661 and 688 and who died at Armagh in 700. The *Life* was written some time between 661 and 700. Apart from Cogitosus's *Life of Brigit* it is the earliest piece of Irish hagiography. Muirchú calls Cogitosus his 'father' [Preface ii]. This need not be seen as an acknowledgement of paternity but can be viewed merely as a statement of gratitude for intellectual inspiration and the provision of a prototype.

In comparison to the halting and badly-honed style of his hero, Muirchú writes with a certain fluency. He is particularly strong as a story-teller and his anecdotes are gripping, vivid and real. Like Patrick, he is steeped in the Bible, quoting often from the sacred text, especially from the psalter, and using scriptural language. While Patrick is *homo unius libri*, a man versed in only one book, Muirchú is much more widely read. He slips quotations into his narrative from Virgil and Sedulius and shows an acquaintance with Ovid. By no stretch of the imagination, however, can he be described as a first-rate writer. His work in general is pedestrian, rather pedantic and lacking in cohesion.

The *Life* begins with an account of Patrick's origins, capture, slavery, escape and return home. This section of the work is based on a version of the *Confessio* which the author must have had to hand. The next part of the book tells how Patrick planned to go to Rome but got no further than Auxerre, where he stayed with Germanus for thirty or forty years. While there he heard of Palladius and his Irish mission and set out to join Prosper's 'first bishop'. In the very early stages of his journey to Ireland he learned of Palladius's death. Patrick was then ordained by Amathorex as a bishop; Auxilius and Iserninus and others receiving lesser orders on the same day. They all made their way to Ireland via Britain, arriving at the port of *Inber Dee* in what is now Co Wicklow. Next Patrick sailed northwards to make his way to Slemish in a vain attempt to convert his former master, the slave-owner Miliucc. En route to Slemish, he met and baptised Díchu and, when Miliucc burned himself to death rather than accept Christ, Patrick returned to his neophyte at Mag Inis in 'the territory of the Ulaid ... [and] stayed there for many days and travelled around the whole plain. He favoured and loved the district, and the faith began to spread there' [I,12 (iv)]. Patrick's first Easter as a bishop in Ireland was spent in the vicinity of the royal palace at Tara. The work reaches a crescendo at this point with a dramatic confrontation over the lighting of the paschal fire between the pagan King Loiguire and his druids and Patrick and his retinue. Patrick displays to his adversaries the power of Christianity.

The remainder of the work gives us a series of unrelated stories, one of them being an account of how Patrick punished the British king Corictic, 'a persecutor and murderer of Christians' [I,29 (ii)], by turning him into a fox, and another being the history of Patrick's receipt of 'the marvellous and pleasing gift' [I,24 (xv)] from Dáire of 'the city which is now called Armagh'. The book ends with an account of how, during his last days, Patrick attempted unsuccessfully to return to his beloved Armagh to die but expired instead at Saul on 17th March (the year is not specified) when he was one hundred and twenty years of age! Muirchú tells us that his hero was buried at Downpatrick close to the place of his death.

Like all pieces of hagiography, Muirchú's Life tells us something about the period in which it was written. Muirchú's Patrick is a typical hagiographical figure. Kathleen Hughes [1972] has pointed out that there are certain conventions in hagiography: for example, the saint is always severely ascetic; he is often in close harmony with the animal world; and he can pronounce potent curses, so that people disregard him at their peril. Muirchú's Patrick is given to robust self-mortification, spending three or four decades in a monastery in Gaul. His closeness to the animal world is shown in the story about how he saved a fawn from being slaughtered by his companions and kept it and its mother until he could release them into the safety of a wood. Patrick's ability to curse is demonstrated by the fate of the unfortunate Corictic and by his prophecies that none of Loiguire's or Miliucc's descendants would gain royal power. Hughes also says that hagiographers were influenced by the conventions of secular story-telling. This is eminently true of Muirchú's Patrick who is presented as having many of the magical powers of the pagan hero: for instance, he manages to ensure that the chief druid is burned to death and that his own follower, Benignus, is saved in the celebrated conflagration of the house at Tara.

Since the Life is so typical of the hagiographical genre in the respects noted above, its chief value lies in the incidental information it contains with regard to seventh-century life and politics and the hints it may give us regarding Irish society in the almost hidden centuries prior to that. Muirchú's Life cannot then be dismissed as a historical source. It tells us much about the period in which it was composed. The reader may find much of the contents of the book fanciful – Patrick's demise at the age of one hundred and twenty, for example, is hard to swallow – and may be tempted to treat it all with too much scepticism. As well as giving us contemporaneous information about the period in which it was written, it probably also contains pieces of significant data on the role of Palladius in the history of the Church in Ireland, on Patrick's association with Auxerre and the bishops Germanus and Amator, and, perhaps most importantly of all, on the obscure connections between the saint and the Ulaid in the fifth century – crucial in piecing together and completing the jigsaw puzzle that is the historical Patrick.

Tírechán's *Brief Account* has also been edited and translated by both Liam de Paor [1993] and Ludwig Bieler. Bishop Tírechán was a native of Tir-awley, Co Mayo, a place identified by many scholars as the elusive *Silva Focluti* of the *Confessio*, 23. Tirawley had supposedly been incorporated into the confederation of Patrician Churches in Patrick's day. Tírechán wants to give his own local church a respectable pedigree and to link it with Patrick and Armagh which claimed the saint in a special way. And so the author stresses the status of Armagh in the Irish Church and also, since he was a Connachtman, emphasises Patrick's missionary labours in the west of Ireland. Tírechán's work is not a *Life* but a record of Patrick's supposed activities.

He begins by recounting Patrick's captivity, his escape and his travels through Gaul, Italy and the islands in the Tyrrhene Sea (that corner of the Mediterranean between France and Italy). He informs us that Patrick and his Gaulish retinue arrived in Ireland at some islands off the coast of Dublin. He then brings his hero to what is now Co Meath, where one of his first actions is to baptise the infant Benignus and appoint him as his 'heir' [5,iv]. Benignus is described as 'Patrick's successor in the church of Armagh' [5,iv] {Note 2}. Tírechán discusses the arrangements that Patrick made regarding the foundation of churches in Meath and has the saint encounter King Loíguire, who, while sympathetic, never allows himself to be baptised. The *Brief Account* then brings Patrick around much of Ireland, founding churches and appointing clergy for them. Tírechán links the saint with Connacht, Ulster, Leinster and north Munster, as far as Cashel. It is difficult to avoid the conclusion that Patrick's association with these places, for the most part at least, is fictitious. Tírechán too conveniently identifies his hero with all the major centres in the island! The work is of value, however, in that it tells us much about the toponymy and politics of seventh-century Ireland.

Tírechán was not writing in a vacuum. A close reading of the text reveals that he had two written sources: a book in the possession of his master, Bishop Ultán of Ardbraccan in Co Meath, who died in 657, and 'a straight-forward narrative' [III,1 (vii)] which was probably a rudimentary biography of the saint based on the *Confessio*. Tírechán would also seem to have been familiar with the *Confessio* itself and would appear to have had oral information about Patrick which he collected on fact-finding missions around the country.

O'Rahilly, Carney, Binchy and Hughes [1966] all tell us that Tírechán was also somewhat indebted to the anonymous authors of the *Book of the Angel*. Tírechán probably wrote no earlier than 668 and would seem, though a contemporary of Muirchú, to have been uninfluenced by him. It is possible, however, that he wrote a decade or two later than the author of the *Life*. Tírechán is a most worthwhile source for the historian interested in the late seventh century. His work also enshrines the three, all-important *Sayings of Patrick*. Unfortunately, his other references to Patrick tend to confuse rather than enlighten the enthusiast and the *Brief Account* is undoubtedly of much less value than Muirchú's *Life* as a source of information regarding the real Saint Patrick.

Muirchú's *Life* seems to show that the saint's history is somehow tied up with the decline of the Ulaid and the triumph of the Uí Néill. Kathleen Hughes [1972] is of the opinion that the supreme realist Muirchú, as much a seventh-century Armaghman as a churchman, would seem to be intent on acknowledging the superiority of the Uí Néill while not dissociating his hero from the Ulaid. The Uí Néill held sway in Muirchú's native area and so the book reaches its climax at Tara, the Uí Néill royal seat. The king and all his followers owe their conversion to Patrick. The Uí Néill, in Muirchú's eyes, can therefore justly claim Patrick as their patron saint. Muirchú had to fabricate an elaborate account of Patrick's death and burial to 'explain' why the saint did not die and was not buried at Armagh 'which he loved above all places' [II,4] but ended his life at Saul and was interred at Downpatrick, both in Leth Cathail (the Lecale area of Co Down), the heartland of the Ulaid.

How are Patrick's identification with the Ulaid and his supposed simultaneous associations with Armagh in Muirchú best explained? Perhaps the answer lies in Emhain Macha, or Navan Fort, a most important ancient site some two miles west of the modern city of Armagh {Note 3}. Some claim that Emhain Macha was the capital of the Ulaid for hundreds of years; others believe that it was not a royal residence at all but a great cultic centre. Both approaches would actually appear to be correct.

Navan Fort is one of fifty-five Irish rivers, islands, peoples and places that are named in Ptolemy's well-known, second-century Map of Ireland, where it is styled *Isamnion* (or, some suggest, *Regia*). The people in what are now Co Armagh, south Down and Louth are called the *Volunti* (in Greek *Ouolountioi*) by Ptolemy. Linguistic authorities are convinced that these are the Ulaid, the original inhabitants of Ulster.

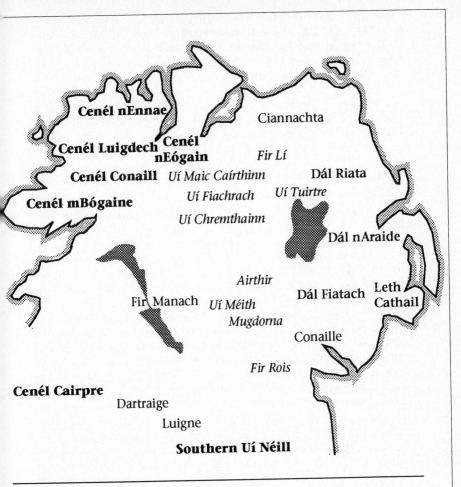

Cenél nEnnae

Cenél Luigdech Cenél
            nEógain

Cenél Conaill   Uí Maic Caírthinn

Cenél mBógaine

Ciannachta

Fir Lí

Dál Riata

Uí Fiachrach   Uí Tuirtre

Uí Chremthainn

Dál nAraide

Airthir

Fir Manach   Uí Méith

Mugdorna

Dál Fiatach   Leth
                Cathail

Conaille

Fir Rois

Cenél Cairpre

Dartraige

Luigne

Southern Uí Néill

Key: **Uí Néill Kingdoms** *Airgialla* Ulaid Others

The Political Geography of the North of Ireland
in the Early Medieval Period

Archaeologists from Queen's University, Belfast, under Dudley Waterman, in 1963-71 discovered evidence of both the religious and secular use of the site {Note 4}. Waterman and his team found evidence of human activity for the last five thousand years. Their most significant discoveries were that it was a Bronze Age royal settlement (for what commoner would have owned a Barbary ape?) and that around 100BC it was the site of an enormous pagan temple. This structure – formed by a ring of large posts, probably roofed, and dominated by a gigantic central totem pole – was forty metres across. Shortly after its construction, it was filled with stones, purposely burned and then covered with sods and earth, possibly so that it would continue forever as a focal point in the otherworld. The whole area, then, was a most important ritual complex.

But where does Patrick fit into the picture? Tradition has it that Emhain Macha was again destroyed in 332 by invaders, led by the three Collas, who broke the power of the Ulaid for good. It may be, however, that the Ulaid were not defeated as early as 332 and that the saint began his mission at Armagh and founded a church there in 444, as the *Annals of Ulster* record. This foundation would have taken place before the Ulstermen were driven out of the area and east of the Bann by the Uí Néill and their allies the Airgialla. At the stage when Muirchú was writing, the Ulaid had become isolated in what is now Co Down and the Airgialla formed a buffer-state subordinate to the Uí Néill. The Uí Néill were predominant in a crescent of territory stretching from the east coast, north of Dublin, to Sligo Bay and thence northwards to Inishowen. In Muirchú's day Armagh was in the territory of the *Airthir*, one of the nine subordinate 'Hostage-givers' to the northern Uí Néill. When exactly they displaced the Ulaid is uncertain. Some modern historians – notably, Francis John Byrne – are of the opinion that the Ulster kingdom was not destroyed until 'as late as 450' and that, 'when Armagh was founded in 444 as the chief church in Ireland, Emhain Macha may still have been the most important political centre.'

The date of the destruction of Emhain Macha is important: on it hinges the connection between Patrick, Emhain Macha and Armagh. Patrick could have chosen Armagh as the site of his main foundation because it was beside the Ulster capital at Emhain Macha (just as Augustine was to choose Canterbury and Aidan was to pick Lindisfarne in their rival missions to the English). An evangelist will, of course, be at his most influential when he is close to the seat of secular power. Maybe Patrick chose Armagh, as Anne Ross suggests, because of its time-honoured links with worship (albeit pagan worship). Or perhaps, as Doctor Stancliffe speculates, it may be that Patrick established a Church close to Emhain Macha because it was the supreme pagan centre in the north and he wanted to confront heathenism head-on, where it was at its most vigorous and challenging. However, as we cannot date the fall of Emhain Macha with any degree of confidence, it is impossible to prove conclusively that there was any relationship between it, Patrick and the Church at Armagh.

Francis John Byrne's claim that Emhain Macha was destroyed as late as 450 has caused some debate but not nearly so much as his assertion that Armagh was established by Patrick in the mid-fifth century as the primatial see. Many scholars have examined the evidence on the subject and have reached the same conclusion as Tomás Ó Fiaich: that Armagh was almost certainly founded by Saint Patrick as his pre-eminent Church in Ireland. Others do not concur. James Carney, for instance, argues that Patrick 'did not found Armagh and was never bishop there.' Some authorities are quite happy to accept the 444 date for the foundation of Armagh but a number of historians are sceptical of this particular entry in the *Annals of Ulster* and regard it as an interpolation. However, other references in the *Annals* seem to afford Armagh a pre-eminent position in the Irish Church and strongly support the 'traditional' identification of the saint with the see {Note 5}.

And what light do other sources throw on this vexed question? The *Book of the Angel*, a pseudo-Patrician document in the *Book of Armagh*, attempts to stress and support, or rather 'to state', Armagh's claims to primacy in the Irish Church. This work has also come under the careful scrutiny of Doctor Bieler. His edition of the Latin text and a translation are to be found in his great work on Patriciana already referred to above. Kathleen Hughes's rendition of the work can be read in *The Church in Early Irish Society* (London, 1966; pp 275 - 281).

The *Book of the Angel* underlines the prestige of Patrick and his successors because of the saint's role in bringing Christ to the people of Ireland. It is a statement in hagiographical terms of the claims of Armagh, as to both territorial and ecclesiastical supremacy. The actual document is framed by an account – probably later than the central text – which tells of how Patrick was granted the honours due to him and his heirs in the see of Armagh by an angel. Kathleen Hughes [1966] was of the opinion that the work, as we now have it, is hardly earlier than the eighth century, for much of its ecclesiastical language belongs to a period later than that of the authors of the *Life of Patrick* and the *Brief Account*. Nevertheless, she observes that, since Tírechán was familiar with some of its claims, the author of the *Brief Account* had before him 'the main sources on which the

Book of the Angel is based'. Richard Sharpe's suggestion that the anonymous compilers of the *Book of the Angel* were 'busy around 640 or 650' may then be substantially correct. John Gwynn's view that the *Book of the Angel* has to be placed in the last quarter of the eighth century is very much a minority opinion.

After a short preamble, the document opens with an account of the angel appearing to Patrick and declaring that God had granted a number of privileges 'to his city'[7 and 8], including an extension of its *termonn*. The Irish word *termonn* means the area immediately subject to an abbot over which he exercises direct government, as distinct from the *paruchia* over which he has only indirect suzerainty {Note 6}. Patrick then begs for further honours, which must be understood to have been granted also. He asks, for example, that he might have the right to tax all 'the free churches of the provinces ... and likewise all monasteries of cenobites' [13]. The second half of the document details the privileges of Armagh and its *praesul* ('leader') [17]. The *Book of the Angel* states that the claims of Armagh – particularly to 'precedence ... over all the churches and monasteries of all the Irish' [18] – are based primarily on the fact that an angel had announced to its founder that God had established Armagh as his supreme church in Ireland. It declares, furthermore, that the place itself is hallowed for it possesses relics of Saints Peter, Paul, Stephen, Laurence and others, including some of the members of Patrick's retinue, and a linen towel steeped 'in the most holy blood of Jesus Christ' [19]. The document concludes with a set of decrees establishing the ecclesiastical court of Armagh as the supreme court of appeal in the island, from which resort can be made only to Rome. The work purports to have been signed by Auxilius, Patricius, Secundinus and Benignus.

It should be obvious that this book is an unapologetic attempt to justify the claims of Armagh. It is shameless propaganda. A number of dubious features should be noted. Its reference to Armagh as the highest court of appeal in the Irish Church is not supported by any of the information we possess from surviving pieces of early Irish law. Certain sections [verses 15 and 16] of the work have undoubtedly been added by a redactor. The order of the 'signatories' is suspect for Patrick's name comes after that of Auxilius. The presence of Benignus's name on the document along with that of Patrick, who was several decades his senior, is also suspicious.

Tomás Ó Fiaich, however, holds that Armagh's case does not rest simply on these above-mentioned writings. He examines all the sources which deal with Patrick and Armagh's claim to primacy and

Richard Sharpe credits him with being 'fairly rigorous in his criticism of them'. One of these is a letter, preserved for us by Bede, which can be very accurately dated to 640, from John IV, Pope-Elect, and other Roman clergy, to ecclesiastics of the northern part of Ireland, all of them supporters of the Irish party in the Easter controversy. This letter places Tomméne, bishop and abbot of Armagh, first in the list of clerics addressed, including the abbots of Clonard, Nendrum, Bangor and Iona. From this it may be possible to deduce that by 640 Rome had given recognition to Armagh's premier position within the Irish Church and that this pre-eminence was accorded Armagh because it was Patrick's own special Church. Sharpe is not convinced and believes that Rome at this time was ill-informed about the state of the Irish Church and that the Roman letter merely reflects the order of the signatures on the letter received from Ireland, a missive on which 'the bishop of Armagh placed his own signature at the head of the list', as part of his Church's policy of aggrandisement.

In his endeavour to link Patrick with Armagh, Cardinal Ó Fiaich uses a number of other sources: for example, the list of ecclesiastical and civil rulers, headed by Flann, abbot-bishop of Armagh from 688-714, who attended the assembly at Birr in 697 (a source which surely weakens Sharpe's arguments against the 640 Roman letter); the ninth-century *Tripartite Life of Patrick* which has two sections of northern material dealing with the activities of the saint in Armagh and its environs; and a verse in the *Additamenta (Supplementary Material)* in the Book of Armagh which records that, when Aed of Sleibte wished to join his church to the confederation of Patrician Churches, he went to Segéne, abbot of Armagh from 661-688, and affiliated 'his kin and his church to Patrick till Doom' [16,i]. But each of these sources has the same basic failing: they all tend to reflect Armagh's position at the date of their compilation and thus do not prove that Patrick founded Armagh.

It would seem that by the late seventh century attention was being focused on Patrick's writings and that certain parties would have found it convenient to be associated with his name. (And one of these parties may have been the Church of Armagh trying to assert its influence over the monastic *paruchiae*.) Although there is a wealth of later tradition linking the name of Patrick with that of Armagh, the saint himself does not give any indication that he established it as his see nor is there any indisputable contemporary evidence for the association. We cannot, as Tomás Ó Fiaich requests, accept without question that, because Patrick was familiar with the diocesan system in Britain and Gaul, he must have set up a permanent base for his Church; nor can we consent unequivocally to the claims of Armagh simply because they have been made so vociferously and for such a long time. Nevertheless, we find it impossible to dissociate Patrick's name from that of Armagh.

Although Saint Patrick is not mentioned in the writings of Columban and Bede, two of the major sources for our period, and although he receives only one brief and unrevealing mention in Adomnan's *Life of Columba* [the 'Second Preface', 3a], there is elsewhere ample and incontestable evidence of the widespread cult of Patrick in the seventh century. Muirchú and Tírechán are, of course, the chief exponents of this approach. But others were also giving Patrick special recognition. The priest Cummian, for instance, in his letter to Segéne, abbot of Iona, dated 632 or 633, refers to the saint as *papa noster* ('our father'); no mean recognition, indeed, from a prominent *Romanus*, a seventh-century pro-Roman churchman opposed to the independent approaches of certain – mostly northern – Irish clerics! The *Antiphonary of Bangor*, compiled in the 680s also designates Patrick *magister Scottorum* ('the teacher of the Irish)' and early *Lives* of Saint Brigit have the Leinster abbess acknowledge his seniority and receive his patronage.

It seems, then, that Patrick's contribution to the spread of the faith in Ireland was widely recognised in seventh-century Ireland. He may not have been responsible for the conversion of the 'Five-Fifths' of the island but his was seen as the major evangelisation and seventh-century churchmen felt that he merited the title 'apostle of Ireland'. At the same time some of those same churchmen were claiming that the saint also deserves to be called 'Patrick of Armagh'. If Armagh 'hi-jacked' the saint, then this must have been done between his death (no earlier than 461) and the middle of the seventh century. It is difficult to avoid Doctor Byrne's conclusion that the saint founded Armagh in the mid-fifth century before the collapse of the Ulaid and that, when the Uí Néill and their allies (the Airgialla) triumphed, he moved his seat to Downpatrick. For a number of decades Patrick's successors had no difficulty in linking themselves with him but felt alienated from those who had displaced the Ulaid at Armagh. Gradually, in the fifth century, a *modus vivendi* was reached and, 'the Ulaid acknowledged Armagh's primacy long before they became reconciled even to an Uí Néill high-kingship'. Thereafter the 'successor of Patrick' and the 'bishop of Armagh' were one and the same person in the see which the saint had founded. The evidence in the Annals and in the sources from the seventh century on permit us, we feel, to refer to the saint as the apostle of Ireland and as Patrick of Armagh.

A medieval carving of St Patrick from Faughart, Co Louth
Photo: courtesy National Museum of Ireland

Notes

1. Scholars have found it difficult to reconstruct Muirchú's *Life* because no complete manuscript survives. Versions of the *Life* are preserved in four manuscripts: the *Book of Armagh* which was compiled before the year 807 and is now preserved in Trinity College, Dublin; *Reg. 64*, a folio in three hands and dating from the eleventh century, in the Bibliothèque Royale in Brussels; *Nat. ser. noav 3642*, two fragments written by an Anglo-Saxon scribe in the late eighth century, and now housed in the National-bibliothek in Vienna; and *cap. 77* which is of the thirteenth century and is to be found in the Library at Novara.

2. There are two other allusions to this church in the *Brief Account*: references to 'a paten in Patrick's church at Armagh' [22 i] and to the education and ordination, 'with Patrick ... at Armagh' [33 ii], of Medbu, a Corkman.

3. Emhain Macha, along with Armagh or Ard Macha, gets part of its name from the pagan Celtic goddess Macha. It is a huge, almost circular enclosure of more than twelve acres on the summit of a low but commanding glacial hill. The complex is about three hundred and seventy-five metres in diameter.

4. The King's Stables, Lough na Shade and Haughey's Fort, all close to Emhain Macha, have also divulged interesting artifacts to archaeologists and others. Towards the end of the 1700s, Lough na Shade, a sacred lake, gave up to a labourer toiling on its banks four decorated, bronze devotional trumpets (one of which has survived) and a number of human and animal skeletal remains from pre-Christian sacrifices. Archaeologists have in recent times discovered sacrificial debris at the King's Stables.

5. The *Annals of Ulster* are the earliest and most reliable of all the Irish chronicles. The most recent edition and translation is that of the late Seán Mac Airt and Gearóid Mac Niocaill, *The Annals Of Ulster* (Dublin, 1983). Doctor Liam de Paor points out that the section of the Annals dealing with our period received its present form, probably in the monastery of Bangor, early in the eighth century. Its list of bishops/abbots of Armagh comes apparently from diptychs, prayers in the Mass for prominent deceased people, in use in the church of Armagh. While the annalistic entry recording the establishment of Armagh in 444 may be suspicious when read in isolation, it may be more useful when taken along with the obits of the early (supposed) bishops of Armagh. The deaths of the following putative bishops or abbots of Armagh in the two centuries after the record of the foundation of the church are listed in the *Annals of Ulster*: Benignus (467), Iarlaithe (481), Cormac (497), Dubthach (513), Ailill (526 and 536), Dáuíd of Farannán (551 and 553), Feidlimid (578), Cairlén (588), Eochu (598), Senach (610), and Mac Laisre (623). Two of these records – the 497 and 551 entries – link the diocese of the deceased prelate with Saint Patrick. While the 551 record, which gives Dáuíd of Farannán the primacy by calling him the 'legate of all Ireland', is an interpolation and therefore possibly spurious, the statement for 497 is mostly in the main hand of the manuscript. Unfortunately, while it states that Cormac was the 'successor of Patrick' in the main text, its identification of him as 'bishop of Ard Macha' is in another hand. Benignus is not associated in the reference to him with Armagh but is described as 'successor of Patrick'. Iarlaithe is not called Patrick's successor but is described as 'third bishop of Ard Macha'. These early allusions to Patrick and/or his successor and/or Armagh probably reveal what Professor Francis John Byrne calls the 'great confusion' exhibited by the annalistic entries 'as to the immediate successors of Patrick in the see of Armagh.'

6. Eoin MacNeill remarks that the *termonn* of Armagh as here circumscribed extends to the outer bounds of Airgialla, Dál nAraide and Ulaid but excludes the territories of the northern and southern Uí Néill and of Dál Riata.

CHAPTER FIVE

Irish Monasticism

'Whoever loves Christ,
follows the steps of Christ.'

[Poem by Saint Columban to Sethus]

Christ's counsel of perfection – 'Go, sell what you possess and give to the poor, and you will have treasure in heaven; and come, follow me' (Mt 19:21) – has influenced his followers since he himself was on earth.

Apostles like Saint Paul advocated prayerful self-discipline and mortification, and from a very early period in the history of the Church heroic souls practised private asceticism: that is, they devoted themselves to intense prayer and severe penitential exercises in their own homes.

As the possibilities of martyrdom receded, with an end to the active persecution of the Church, men and women looked for opportunities to live austerely and contemplatively. Saint Anthony (251-356) was one of the first of the so-called Desert Fathers, those men who took the command of Jesus at its most literal, giving away their possessions, going into the Egyptian desert and living lives of prayer, work, self-denial and solitude. Initially these ascetics would seem to have been totally isolated individuals but gradually what is known as the eremitical institution developed, where hermits came together occasionally to pray and receive direction from a leader.

Out of this movement evolved coenobitism or what we call the religious life. The essence of coenobitism is dwelling in community, which demands that those living in it draw up a rule to follow. For these early monks, the main values to be observed were poverty, chastity and obedience. The chief proponent of coenobitism was Pachomius (c 290-346) founder of the monastery of Tabennisi in the Thebaid, near Denderah on the right bank of the Nile. From Egypt, monasticism spread throughout the Christian world, progressing at first in the east, into Palestine, Syria, Mesopotamia and Greece, and then in the west into Africa, Italy and Gaul. Some of the most famous early monasteries in France were Martin's foundations at Ligugé and Marmoutiers just outside Tours, John Cassian's abbey of Saint Victor at Marseilles, and Saint Honoratus's foundation on the tiny island which now bears his name in Les Iles Lérins just off Cannes.

From France, the monastic movement spread into Britain where Ninian, the early fifth-century apostle of the Picts in what is now Scotland, established a monastery at Whithorn or *Candida Casa*. It is on the coast of Galloway, fairly close to the modern port of Stranraer. It was here that the most famous monastic founders from the northern half of Ireland received their training: Enda of Aran, Tighernach of Clones, Eoghan or Eugene of Ardstraw, Finnian of Moville and Coirpre of Coleraine.

Monasticism flourished similarly in Wales, where its first most important advocate was Illtud, founder of the monastery of Caldey Island. Among his disciples were Samson of Dol, Cadoc, Gildas and David. Tradition has it that two of these men had associations with Ireland. Samson (died c 565) is said to have visited Ireland before going to Brittany. Gildas (c 500-570), who would seem to have received his initial inspiration to become a monk from Cadoc, was also closely associated with Ireland. He is of major significance in the history of Irish monasticism. John Ryan [1931] says that 'it is to him, more than to any other, that the distinctive monastic form assumed by the Church in Ireland is chiefly due'. Gildas may have visited Ireland. He saw monasticism as the perfect way of following Christ and perhaps thereby encouraged Irish people to adopt the religious life. He also advocated that no authentic religious rule should be outlawed and so created a climate in Ireland in which numerous, distinct monastic rules evolved, and a spirit of toleration of differences emerged. There were close links between the southern half of Ireland and Wales and it seems that many of the early Irish monastic founders from Leinster and Munster were trained in that country, especially by Illtud at Caldey Island and David at Mynyw. Among these famous Irishmen were Finnian of Clonard, Aidan of Ferns, Senan of Scattery Island and Brendan of Clonfert.

Monasticism in Ireland came, then, indirectly from France and directly from Britain, but definitely along two distinct veins, one from northern Britain and the other from Wales. It arrived in Ireland in the generation after Saint Patrick, but soon over-shadowed the diocesan system which he had introduced. Patrick, of course, would seem to have admired the religious life, encouraged some people to practise severe asceticism [see, for instance, *Confessio* 41 and 42] and may even himself have been for a time a monk.

A number of theories have been advanced as to why monasticism in Ireland came to rival the normal ecclesiastical constitution of the Church. In the sixth and seventh centuries, the Irish Church was distinctly monastic in character and constitution and the diocesan system seems to have been partially submerged by it. Why did this development take place? Liam de Paor is of the opinion that the great plague of the 540s contributed crucially to the growth of the monastic federations. The older (diocesan) churches in Ireland would seem to have had close links with France – 'the worst source of infection' – and 'would have been, as it were, singled out by the pestilence. This visitation must thus explain in part the decline or disappearance of many of the earliest churches' and, we might add, the rise of the monastic *paruchiae* ('the monastic families of particular founders' or 'the confederations of monasteries all owing their existence to the activities or inspiration of individual monastic saints').

Kathleen Hughes [1972] also addresses the problem. She advances three possible answers to the question. First, Ireland being a barbarian region, without any of the Roman imperial structures out of which the typical continental diocese developed, had the opportunity to evolve in its own unique fashion. Monasticism was to prove most attractive to Irishmen in the sixth century and they were able to permit the phenomenon to grow in a way which it could not in Europe and Britain. Secondly, two native institutions, kin and kingship, influenced the organisational growth of the Irish Church. Irish inheritance laws kept land within the family. As monasticism developed, abbots seem to have followed secular legal practices when they appointed their successors and very often abbots of the Irish monasteries were all of the same family. Celtic customs regarding inheritance and kinship would seem to have favourably affected the growth of monasticism, though they do not fully explain the Irish system, as the same principles might have been applied to episcopal succession and diocesan control. Kingship, the other significant indigenous institution, must also have influenced the trend towards monasticism. As we have said before, Celtic Ireland was made up of some one hundred and fifty autonomous kingdoms or *tuatha*. These were usually linked in alliances and there were kings and superior kings in the country. Just as in the secular world some rulers were over-kings, dominating confederations of kingdoms, so in the Irish Church, some abbots and monasteries were dominant in confederations of religious houses. Hughes sees a striking parallel between the monastic *paruchia* and secular overlordship. Thirdly, the eventual paramountcy of the monastic *paruchia* must in some way be explained by economics. Fifth-century dioceses were of necessity limited regarding endowments as they would seem to have been financed by the farms of the pagan sanctuaries which they replaced. The monastic movement was popular, however, and would seem to have had almost unbounded opportunities for growth. Whole families could join monasteries and convents and could donate their lands to these institutions. The monastic *paruchia* had therefore 'almost unlimited powers of expansion' and developed accordingly. These views go some way towards explaining the spectacular development of monasticism in Ireland.

This chapter, so far, has been rather abstract and has made no attempt to capture the flavour of Irish monastic life. Irish monasticism was popular, gripping thousands so that they devoted themselves to a way of life which would seem to the outsider most unattractive. What was this lifestyle? What was the daily routine of the typical monk or nun? What were the conditions in which they lived?

Irish monasteries were unimpressive architecturally. Normally built inside ring-forts, like the more secure domestic accommodation in the country at the time, they consisted of clusters of little huts around a small church. Traditionally, it has been held that in the typical Celtic monastery these huts would have been a kitchen, a dining-room, a library/scriptorium, a wash-house, a guest-house and several cells {Note 1}. Usually each monk would have had his own cell but it is known that in some monasteries as many as nine monks shared quarters. Throughout most of Ireland, all these buildings would have been made of wood and wattle-and-daub: impermanent structures which have disappeared without trace. Occasionally, however, when timber was unavailable, stone was used and so some early monastic buildings, like those on Skellig Michael, Innismurray and Duvillaun off the Kerry, Sligo and Mayo coasts respectively, have survived. In each enclosure there was a cemetery in which deceased monks were buried and in which local kings would also seem to have found a last resting-place. Clonmacnois, for instance, on the east bank of the Shannon, is the burial-place of the kings of Connacht, the great kingdom just across the river, and at Glendalough several local rulers have been interred.

The standard work on Irish ecclesiastical architecture is Harold G Leask's *Irish Churches and Monastic Buildings*. Leask devotes the first six chapters of his work to an examination of the few stone buildings of the early Irish Church which have survived along the treeless western seaboard. One of the most interesting of these historic monuments is Saint Molaise's island monastery on Innismurray. This site is surrounded by our 'most complete monastic cashel remaining.' Erected in the seventh or eighth century, the walls of the cashel rise to-day to a maximum of some thirteen feet. They are between seven and fifteen feet in thickness at the base and 'enclose a space broadly egg-shaped and measuring, internally, about 175 feet in length and 135 feet in breadth.' This enclosure is subdivided by lesser walls. Several internal flights of stone steps give access to the wall-tops and there are a number of entrances to the complex, the main one being at the northern end of the boundary-wall.

Several buildings have survived inside the cashel, the most notable being some beehive cells. Beehive cells (or *clocháin*) were erected using the ancient technique of corbelling. This is the method by which a vaulted building is constructed by laying a succession of stone courses on top of each other inwards from all sides until they meet at a central cap-stone. This technique is eminently suited to the erection of small circular buildings. It is not as successful when applied to the building of rectangular, unmortared churches entirely in stone. Early Irish church architects designed and erected oratories using this method, the Gallarus Oratory (Co Kerry) being the most famous. Saint Macdara's Church off the Galway coast was of similar construction. It is interesting because it has *antae* or side walls projecting slightly beyond the line of the gable walls. Some early stone churches, the Oratory at Kilmalkedar (Co Kerry) for instance, are crowned by ornaments known as gable finials. The *antae* and finials served no practical purpose and would seem to be decorative 'translations into stone' of prominent features in timber buildings. These historic monuments, the top stones of several High Crosses, sarcophagi like Saint Muiredach's mortuary house at Banagher (Co Derry), and an ornament in the *Book of Kells*, help us to appreciate what the typical early wooden oratory in an average Irish monastery of our period would have looked like.

Beehive Cells on Skellig Michael, Co Kerry
Photo: courtesy Office of Public Works, Dublin

The government of each monastery was rigidly hierarchical. The chief authority was the abbot, to whom absolute obedience was given. He was advised by a number of older monks who were called the *seniores* and was assisted by a vice-abbot who was a sort of dean of discipline-cum-bursar. Other officials in a monastery were a guest-master, a cook, a messenger who kept contact with the outside world, a master of novices, teachers and a layman who acted as land-steward.

The daily life of the typical Irish monk was characterised by its austerity. Much of his day was spent in prayer – private contemplation but, above all, communal prayer – punctuated by periods of manual work, study, eating and sleep. Monks had to survive on the bare minimum of sleep and never had more than two meals a day. In the stricter monasteries only one meal, at three o'clock in the afternoon, was allowed. Fasting was a severe imposition and the pangs of hunger a real trial. Food was of the most Spartan quality. Some abbots demanded that their monks be vegetarian; others allowed fish and seabirds (which were then considered piscine) in the diet; and a few would appear to have permitted the consumption of flesh meat. The chief articles of food in all monasteries were bread and vegetables. However, even to our modern, self-indulgent way of thinking, early Celtic monks had a surprisingly attractive liquid diet. They were allowed water, of course, but beer was also provided and wine on feast days. During three periods each year – the three Irish seasons of Lent: our Advent, our Lent, and on the forty days immediately after Pentecost – and on Wednesdays and Fridays each week, fasting was intensified and dishes were made less appetising in quality and smaller in quantity. Monks who were aged or infirm, however, were always given somewhat more satisfying dishes.

Since monks were vowed to poverty, their clothing was basic. We have little detailed knowledge of this particular aspect of monastic life but we do know that monks wore an inner garment called a *tunica* and an outer robe, the *casula,* which was made of wool and had a hood. In winter monks wore cloaks. Irish monks were allowed to change their clothes at night. They wore sandals and, when journeying, carried staffs. Since they lived in community, great emphasis was placed on personal hygiene and monks were expected to wash frequently. Monks were not clothes-conscious. They lived to please God by the inner beauty of their lives and their personal appearance was unimportant. All they wanted to satisfy were their essential needs.

Silence was demanded in Celtic monasteries and the monk was encouraged to speak only when it was necessary or useful. He was also advised to speak only with prudence. This rule was insisted upon during meals when spiritual reading took the place of casual conversation, with one of the brethren acting as a public reader.

The monk was meant never to be idle at any time during the day. When he was not praying, eating or sleeping he had to be at work. All monks were expected to do some physical work. This would have been farm work mostly, as the monk was supposed to help provide for the needs of the community. It would also have involved the upkeep of the monastic buildings and certain domestic tasks, like cooking, baking and waiting at table. Monks were also directed towards academic pursuits. Novices devoted much of their time to learning and some of the more scholarly of their older colleagues were employed as their teachers. Latin was taught as a means of gaining access to the sacred scriptures, which were obviously all-important to the religious.

Scriptural exegesis was regarded as the highest form of learning. Irish monks studied many Old Testament books (but notably Genesis, Job, the Psalms, Isaiah, Ezekiel and the Song of Songs), all four Gospels, the most popular of which was Matthew, and much of the rest of the New Testament. They were also interested in the Apocrypha and had what amounted to a fascination with uncanonical works such as the Book of the Jubilees, the Gospel according to Peter and the Gospel of Saint James. For their scripture studies they also read the works of several of the great writers of Christian antiquity and were heavily dependent upon such Fathers as Jerome, Ambrose and Augustine.

There were two main schools of exegesis in Ireland: the allegorical and the literalist. The former, which prevailed in Ireland, strove to discover hidden meanings in the sacred text. The latter commented on the primary meaning of particular passages. From the late sixth century onwards, the Vulgate translation of the Bible was predominant in Ireland but, even then, earlier versions of the sacred book survived, especially the Gallican edition of the Psalms. Reverence for the word of God is shown most eloquently by the magnificent copies of certain parts of the Bible which have survived: the *Cathach* (*Battle Reliquary*), the *Book of Durrow*, the *Lindisfarne Gospels* and, above all, the priceless *Book of Kells*. Irish monks were skilled copyists and each monastery had its own scriptorium. It was in Ireland that a completely new approach to the production of books emerged. Until the flowering of the Celtic Church, a book was seen as a means of preserving a message and nothing more. The Irish copyists convinced the world that books themselves should be things of beauty, paying homage through their artistry to the message they contained and simultaneously elevating the reader.

Scholar-monks did not confine themselves to work on the sacred scriptures. Kenney tells us that they also produced hymns, religious poems, prayers, martyrologies, sermons, liturgical material, hagiographical works, calendars, annals and chronicles, letters, voyage and vision tales, prophecies, Latin grammars and treatises of a scientific nature ('chiefly astronomical, computistical and geographical writings').

One other area studied and contributed to by Irish monks was primitive church law. Irish monks studied monastic rules, the canons and the penitentials {Note 2}. The rules were all-important for the monk since they were the guidelines on which he based his daily life and practice. All the major monastic founders seem to have drawn up some type of rule. Many of these are rudimentary in the form in which we now have them but Columban's *Monks' Rule* and his *Community Rule* are comprehensive and informative. The *Monks' Rule* has come down to us in two editions: a ten-chapter version and a fourteen-chapter version. It states the principles of the ascetic life: by strict obedience shall the monk show his love of God and neighbour; only through silence shall he achieve recollection; he shall mortify himself by eating little and poorly; he shall practise poverty, humility, chastity and discretion. The *Rule* gives detailed directions regarding the recitation of the Divine Office, saying that it must be celebrated during 'six hours': at the third (*terce*), sixth (*sext*) and ninth (*none*) hours of the day, at nightfall (*vespers*), at midnight (*vigil*) and in the early morning (*matins*). Columban's system was unique to his own monasteries. There is no evidence that everywhere in Ireland the number of hours was the same. Of course, one should expect variety rather than uniformity in the characteristically diversified Irish Church. Columban's *Community Rule* sets out the usual punishments for failures to observe the Rule: for example, a monk who spoke loudly and unnecessarily was penalised by having to keep silent for a certain length of time or by having to accept fifty (token?) slaps.

The basic principles of monasticism and all aspects of Irish monastic life belong originally to other countries and to another time. Monasticism originated in fourth-century Egypt. There the monk's day was divided into periods of prayer, study and manual work. There the monk was encouraged to fast and live on one meal a day. There, too, obedience was stressed. When monasticism was brought to France it was very obviously indebted to Egyptian prototypes. But, while the community at Lérins owed much to Egyptian coenobitism – practising poverty, chastity, obedience, fasts, vigils and Bible reading – certain developments can be seen. The monks at Lérins placed greater emphasis on solitude and their liturgies and especially their hymns were well in advance of more primitive eastern practices. Most important of all, however, was the stress that Honoratus of Lérins and his followers laid on study. It is possible that Saint Patrick visited Lérins. If this tradition is correct, then that monastery had a seminal influence on Irish Christianity. We can be certain, at any rate, that when monasticism began to take root in Ireland, Lérins contributed significantly, if indirectly, through British monasteries like Caldey Island and British monks like Cadoc and Gildas.

Irish monasticism, thus, was not an innovation but was derived from earlier sources – the primitive religious houses of Egypt, the monastery of Lérins, and some of the fifth-century foundations in Britain. Although derivative, however, Irish monasticism was to a certain extent original: original in the way it combined elements from earlier institutions and in the emphasis it placed on some rather than others of these elements. The first significant feature of Celtic monasticism was, as Ryan [1931] says, its 'combination of apostolical and anchoretical ideals'. While seeking the peace of the cloister and striving for asceticism, the Celtic monk, at least when he left Ireland, was prepared to engage in pastoral and missionary work. It may be that Saint Martin of Tours influenced this particular trend.

Another noteworthy characteristic of Irish monasticism was the harsh austerity it imposed. Severe asceticism was demanded of the Irish monk, more than was expected of monks elsewhere. When this unsparing discipline is combined with intense study (inspired, doubtless, as much by the native schools which preceded Christianity as by the emphasis on scholarship at Lérins) we have a unique combination. Finally, Irish monasticism was original in the prominence it afforded its abbots in the government of the Irish Church. Abbots exercised an enormous influence upon the Church in Ireland for most of our period {Note 3}. This situation arose for two reasons: the popularity of monasticism; and reaction to the scandalous lives of many of the bishops abroad.

Irish monasticism was, then, indebted to the monastic movement elsewhere, but an institution in its own right. It was to survive for some seven hundred years, the last four centuries of which were to see it absolutely predominant in the Church in Ireland. The *Rule* of Saint Benedict (c480-c546) came ultimately to replace it in Europe because it was comparatively mild, comprehensive, legislated for, and supported by the Holy See. But the Irish system survived at home. When it was finally replaced in Ireland, it was superseded not by the moderate Benedictine rule but, in many of the ancient monasteries, by the more severe rule of the Cistercians which was itself rather akin to Celtic monasticism. There are a number of Cistercian houses in Ireland to-day and so Irishmen can still associate themselves with the traditions of their Fathers.

Notes:

1. Recent modern archaeological investigations have revealed that the buildings in certain Columban foundations were somewhat different in size, importance and function from those in the accepted monastic complex. The reader may wish to consult A D S Macdonald's Aspects of the Monastery and Monastic Life in Adomnan's Life of Columba.

2. The penitentials and the canons are treated of more fully in Chapter Ten.

3. We do not agree, however, with the 'traditional' perception that bishops were to all intents and purposes subordinate to the heads of monastic paruchiae and that their role was restricted to administering the sacraments. We explain our reasons for this approach in Chapter Ten.

CHAPTER SIX

Some Famous Monastic Founders

'...and there, in perfect subjection,
patience, and obedience,
he learned, loved, and practised
knowledge, wisdom, chastity,
and every good disposition
of spirit and soul,
as was his heart's desire,
with great fear
and love of God,
in goodness and
simplicity of heart,
a virgin in body and in spirit.'

[Muirchú]

S everal of the early Irish monastic founders who had received
their training at either *Candida Casa* or in Wales returned home
towards the end of the fifth century. We propose dealing in chronological order (by year of death) with the careers of some of these
saints and with the histories of a number of other renowned con-
tributors to the growth of Celtic monasticism. We shall also treat of
four famous female religious. Of necessity, this chapter will take the
form of an extended litany.

Búite of Monasterboice
Monasterboice, with its splendid high crosses and round tower, so
popular with the modern tourist, is, despite the sophistication of
the remains to be seen there to-day, one of the earliest Celtic monasteries in Ireland. It was founded about the year 500 by Búite, a
member of the Ciannachta, a sept which had branches in Munster
and in parts of what are now Co Louth and Co Derry. Born in Munster
and trained in Britain, Búite established his monastery in family territory just north of the modern town of Drogheda. Tradition has it

that the saint died in 521. He was probably quite an aged man at the time of his death and so presumably would have been born in the middle decades of the preceding century. This supposition is supported by the legend that his parents had to bring him a long distance for baptism, as priests were very scarce in the country at that time, and by the fact that he was a bishop as well as being an abbot, a situation which would have been more likely at an early stage in the Irish Church. John Ryan points out that the name Monasterboice preserves a primitive form of the Irish version of the Latin word *monasterium* ('monastery'). It is probably no coincidence that the modern Irish word *muintir* ('a household, family, associates and community') is rooted in the same Latin term. The early Irish monks would have stressed the community aspect of their lives rather than the fact that they lived in a mere complex of buildings. (In the sterile twentieth century, we use the term 'monastery' to describe the edifice rather than the community it houses!) Monasterboice had close associations with the monastery of Llandaff in Wales. It flourished until the Middle Ages. Its famous tenth-century West Cross was erected by the abbot Muireadach and one of its abbots in the eleventh century is still remembered for his historical poems. Being too close to the Pale, Monasterboice lost influence after the Normans established themselves in Ireland.

Enda of Aran

Although the most westerly part of the national territory, and geographically and sociologically linked to Connacht, the Aran Islands are actually part of the province of Munster. It was to Inishmore, the largest of the three Aran Islands, that Enda, a member of the same sept as Búite and a native of the territory in which Monasterboice was built, went to found his monastery about 484. From a military background, the son of a mercenary and formerly himself a soldier, Enda trained as a monk at *Candida Casa*. His own foundation was famous for the severity of its rule and for the numerous monastic saints who (supposedly) received some training there. Finnian of Clonard, Brendan of Clonfert, Jarlath of Tuam, Ciaran of Clonmacnois and Colum Cille are all said to have been alumni of this monastery. Enda, who made a great impact, pioneered the monastic movement in Ireland. His work preceded that of the more influential Finnian. It is generally accepted that Enda died around 540.

Finnian of Clonard

Finnian of Clonard is the patriarch *par excellence* of Irish monasticism. His name in Old Irish means 'the fair-haired one'. He was born to a humble family in what is now Co Meath in the later decades of the fifth century and was schooled in the monastic life in Cadoc's monastery at Llangarvan in Wales. Here he became friendly with Cadoc's illustrious pupil Gildas. Columban tells us that Finnian consulted Gildas and it is likely that this great personality influenced the Irish-man enormously. Gildas was convinced that the monastic life was the perfect way of following Christ and so may have been the impetus, through his admirer Finnian, which ultimately brought about the pre-eminence of the monastic institute in Ireland. Finnian founded his own monastery in the Irish midlands at Clonard. Clonard was one of Ireland's greatest monastic schools. Finnian himself is said to have trained numerous disciples, including the so-called 'Twelve Apostles of Ireland': Ciaran of Saiger, Ciaran of Clonmacnois, Brendan of Clonfert, Brendan of Birr, Colum Cille of Derry, Durrow and Iona, Colmán of Terryglass, Molaisse of Devenish, Canice of Aghaboe, Ruadán of Lorrha, Mobhi of Glasnevin, Sinell of Cleenish and Ninidh of Inishmacsaint. Finnian made two unique contributions to the development of Irish monasticism: first, he placed an enormous em-phasis on the value of study; and secondly, he insisted that his more zealous pupils leave Clonard and establish their own monasteries elsewhere. He did not stress austerity to the same extent as did Enda. Hardly a trace of the monastery of Clonard survives to-day. But Finnian has left monuments to himself – though this was never the intention of so humble an ascetic – across Ireland, Britain and western Europe in the remains of the foundations made by his pupils and their followers. Another monument to the saint is probably the *Penitential of Finnian*, the oldest surviving document of its kind in Hiberno-Latin {Note 1}. Finnian died of the plague in 549.

Ciaran of Clonmacnois

Ciaran of Clonmacnois ranks as one of Finnian's outstanding disci-ples. Like his master, he came from an unprivileged background. His father was an immigrant worker from near what is now Larne (Co Antrim), a carpenter who sought work in the west of Ireland. After his novitiate in Clonard and visits to Enda of Aran and Senan of Scattery Island, Ciaran set up a monastery in what we call to-day Co Roscommon before proceeding to Clonmacnois. Here, on the eastern shores of the Shannon, some eleven miles south of the modern town of Athlone, he founded his great monastery. In the sixth century there was little organised traffic in Ireland. The Shannon, however, was a major artery. It was intersected close to Clonmacnois by one of the few main roads of ancient Ireland. Ciaran's monastery was therefore at a crossroads and in one of the most public places in the country. The kingdom of Connacht lay just across the river and many of the kings of that territory are buried in the monastery graveyard. Some of their tombstones still survive there and are part of a most impressive site visited annually by thousands of pilgrims and tourists. Ciaran is said to have died in 555, at the age of thirty-three, privileged to emulate his Saviour to the end {Note 2}.

Brendan of Clonfert

Brendan the Navigator was another of the 'Twelve Apostles of Ireland'. He was born in the border-region between what are now the Counties of Kerry and Limerick. His father was called Findlug (obviously at the very least the son of a pagan since his name honours the pagan god Lugh). His mother was called Cara. He was trained by a local bishop named Erc and by several well-known figures of the sixth-century Church: Saint Ita, Saint Jarlath, Saint Enda of Aran and Saint Finnian of Clonard. At some time in his career he spent a period in Wales. He also sojourned in Scotland. There he established churches on the island of Tiree and in Perthshire, and was associated with Colum Cille. In Ireland he founded monasteries on islands in the Shannon and in Lough Corrib and at Clonfert in Co Galway. Clonfert was probably founded in 559. Brendan would appear to have died in either 577 or 583. His place in history is secured because a medieval document, the *Navigatio* (*The Voyage*), bears his name. Some people hold that this odyssey is based on an actual voyage which Brendan made to North America {Note 3}. *The Voyage* was a most influential work in medieval times. Its text survives in some one hundred and twenty manuscripts, some of them in Latin and the others in early forms of modern continental languages. The earliest surviving manuscript dates from the late tenth century. *The Voyage* is usually, and probably correctly, ascribed to a late ninth-century Irish *peregrinus* ('pilgrim' or 'missionary exile') working in the Netherlands or Germany. A fascinating conglomeration of fact, fantasy and plagiarism, its popularity on the continent in the Middle Ages led to a cult of Saint Brendan there and means that the name of a comparatively obscure sixth-century Irish monk survives in the name of a thriving city in Germany, Brandenburg. For more immediate reasons, the saint's name also survives in the toponymy – Brandon Head, for instance – of his native south-west Munster.

Canice of Aghaboe

This Irish Pict, the son of a bard and a native of the Dungiven/Limavady area of Co Derry, was yet another of Finnian's disciples. On leaving Clonard, he spent some time with Mobhi at Glasnevin before going to work as a missionary in Scotland along with his fellow Pict Comgall and his great friend Colum Cille. He accompanied these two on their visit to the Pictish King Bruide at Inverness. Formerly it was held that his knowledge of the language undoubtedly made him a most useful missionary in Pictland. Nowadays it is

Major Monastic
Sites in Early Ireland

Derry

Ardstraw

Bangor
Moville

Inishmacsaint
Devenish
Cleenish

Killeavy

Monasterboice

Tuam

Clonard

Glasnevin

Clonmacnois
Clonfert
Durrow

Lorrha
Birr
Saiger
Kildare

Terryglass

Aran

Clonenagh

Glendalough

Clonfertmulloe
Aghaboe

Scattery Island

Killeedy

Ballyvourney

Cork

Cloyne

accepted that the Irish Picts spoke the same tongue as the other inhabitants of Ireland. He is remembered in Scotland to this day as Saint Kenneth and is credited with founding churches on the islands of Coll, Tiree, Mull and South Uist. He is also associated with Kennoway in Fife. Towards the end of his life he returned to Ireland and set up a monastery at Aghaboe. He is venerated in the midlands where the city of Kilkenny very obviously bears his name. He died in the year 600.

Fintan of Clonenagh

Probably the most austere of all the abbot/founders was Fintan, founder of the monastery of Clonenagh in Leinster. Like so many of the saints mentioned above, he came from a modest background. He was baptised and educated by monks near the modern port of New Ross, Co Wexford. He trained as a monk under Colmán of Terryglass and then founded his own community. His rule was appallingly strict. His monks were not allowed milk or milk products nor were they permitted to use animals like oxen to assist them in their manual work. Fintan was enormously influential in the extended Church since he taught Comgall of Bangor, who in turn trained Columban, the founder of a number of great monasteries on the continent. As we have already noted, Columban drew up two monastic rules, the *Monks' Rule* and the *Community Rule*, and so Fintan had an indirect influence on the development of monasticism in western Europe. Tradition has it that Fintan of Clonenagh died in 603.

Comgall of Bangor

Another Irish Pict, Comgall of Bangor, was a product of Fintan's monastery at Clonenagh. He came from south Antrim and was born about 517. Like Enda, he was the son of a soldier of fortune, a man of no social standing in sixth-century Irish society. Like Enda, too, he would seem to have been a soldier himself in his early manhood. After he left Clonenagh, he may have gone to study for a time under Mobhi at Glasnevin before departing to labour in Scotland. He went with Colum Cille and Canice on their visit to King Bruide of the Picts. He founded his own monastery at Bangor in the Ards Peninsula on his return to Ireland, about the year 555. Comgall combined the austerity of his master Fintan with the scholarship demanded by Finnian at Clonard. This combination meant that Bangor was soon the most significant monastery in the country, producing men of great learning and exemplary self-discipline and dedication. Columban is, of course, the supreme product of this institution. But the monastery also trained notable figures like Gall, the apostle of Switzerland, Maelrubha of Applecross, one of the major evangelists of Scotland, and Malachy, who in later centuries became the great archbishop of Armagh and a canonised saint of the Church. Between 680 and 691 the famed *Antiphonary of Bangor* – described by Kenney as 'one of the very few [western] liturgical books of the seventh century which we possess' – was produced at the monastery founded by Comgall on the southern shore of Belfast Lough. It is said that Comgall died at Bangor in 603.

Kevin of Glendalough

Kevin of Glendalough was born in what is now Co Wicklow. Pious legend has it that he was the nephew of Eugene of Ardstraw, patron of the diocese of Derry. He was initiated into the religious life by three monks who lived near Tallaght, the modern Dublin suburb. He founded a hermitage at Holywood, near Blessington, Co Wicklow. When this did not afford him the isolation he required, he moved to the more remote valley of Glendalough in the same locality. Though seeking isolation, he acquired great influence, for numerous disciples followed him to this lonely spot. It was to meet their needs that the saint reluctantly set up and then ran the monastery at Glendalough. In the centuries after Kevin's death, Glendalough became a veritable monastic city. Its extensive remains, once the centre of a medieval diocese linked with Saint Laurence O'Toole, in their spectacular setting in the middle of the Wicklow mountains, are visited by thousands of native and foreign tourists annually. As Clonmacnois is the burial-place of the kings of Connacht, so Glendalough is the royal cemetery of the kings of Leinster. Kevin is said to have died in 618.

Findbarr of Cork

Just as Colum Cille is the patron of Derry, in the extreme north, Findbarr has tutelage over Cork, on the banks of the Lee, in the far south. He has been venerated there since the sixth century. To-day his name survives both in its original form and in the diminutive Barry. His family was originally from the west of Ireland but his father, a metal worker, migrated to Munster where he found employment in west Cork and where his son was born. His mother is supposed to have been a slave-girl. He was trained as a monk by three obscure ascetics in Leinster and then spent some time on *peregrinatio* ('pilgrimage' or 'missionary exile') in Scotland before moving to his native district where he set up a number of hermitages, at Gougane Barra and Kilclooney, for example, and finally the monastery of Cork. Mary Ryan D'Arcy suggests that Findbarr died about 623. John Ryan believes, however, that it is impossible to say with certainty when the saint died.

Space does not permit us to investigate the careers and contributions of all the notable male saints of the early Irish Church. No mention, for example, has been made of Colmán of Cloyne, a great monastic founder and one of the earliest identifiable poets in the Irish language. Nor has detailed reference been made to Finnian of Moville, Molua of Clonfertmulloe or Mobhi of Glasnevin. It would be unpardonable, however, if we did not at least allude to the work of certain female religious. In his *Confessio*, Patrick expresses great pride in the fact that several Irish women became ascetics. From the earliest times, therefore, the Irish Church has produced and been enriched by women saints. Down through the centuries nuns have been particularly successful in preserving their anonymity and so only a few names and details regarding Irish women religious have survived.

Brigit of Kildare

Of these, the most renowned, of course, is Saint Brigit. She is honoured, along with Patrick and Colum Cille, as one of the three patrons of Ireland. Her feast-day is celebrated on 1st February. The name Brigit derives from the Celtic root *brig* meaning 'exalted'. The *Life of Brigit* by Cogitosus, a mid-seventh-century writer, is the earliest ,surviving piece of hagiography with an Irish provenance. Until the welcome publication, in 1993, of Liam de Paor's excellent translation {Note 4}, this important manuscript had not been edited in the last one hundred years and was accessible only in the collections of the seventeenth-century monk-historian John Colgan and the nineteenth-century scholar J P Migne. It inspired Muirchú in the writing of his *Life of Patrick*. There is what Kenney calls a 'noticeable similarity' between parts of the *Life of Brigit* and the writings of the Armaghman. Cogitosus, himself, was indebted to the author of the *Vita Sancti Samsonis (The Life of Saint Samson)*, probably an even earlier surviving piece of Celtic hagiography. The *Life of Brigit* is useful to the historian because of the valuable contemporary evidence it gives us regarding social and ecclesiastical life and politics at the time it was written: matters which the writer describes as having 'not only heard but seen with our own eyes'. Cogitosus, for instance, gives us the first detailed description of an Irish church-building. His account of this edifice shows that Kildare was a most important institution in his day. Kathleen Hughes [1972] is convinced that Cogitosus's *Life* is one of the products of an active seventh-century scriptorium at Kildare and that the writings from this centre reflect the monastery's growing importance in the religious and secular life of Leinster. The *Life* calls Kildare the 'episcopal and virginal see'. It speaks of Kildare's bishop as the 'chief bishop of the Irish bishops' and of its abbess as 'the abbess whom all the abbesses of the Irish venerate'. For Kathleen Hughes this reveals that Kildare was making the same

claims to metropolitan authority that Armagh was to achieve somewhat later in the century. Regrettably, Cogitosus is unreliable as a primary source regarding his saintly subject. The Celts had a goddess
named Brigit. Many of the attributes of this goddess – and even her
festival at the beginning of spring and the perpetual fire kept burning in her honour – would seem to have been transferred to the cult
and legends surrounding the Christian holy woman of the same
name. We have no doubt, nevertheless, that a nun called Brigit existed. She was born in the mid-fifth century near the royal site of
Croghan in what is now Co Offaly. The daughter of a slave-girl, she
managed, despite intense opposition, to become a nun, and founded
the most important double monastery of Kildare where she was assisted by a bishop called Conlaedh. Double monasteries consisted of
two separate but adjacent houses, one for the nuns and the other for
monks, built around a common chapel. It was the abbess who ruled
both houses. This situation arose from the need the nuns had for
the sacerdotal services of ordained monks and for protection. They
also required help with the heavier kind of work that the female
community was unable to do for itself {Note 5}. According to the
Annals of Ulster, Brigit died in the 520s, 'when in the seventieth year
of her age'. Conlaedh died at the very start of the same decade. Both
Brigit and Conlaedh were, it seems, buried at Kildare under the high
altar in the Great Church.

Gobnet of Ballyvourney, Moninne of Killeavy and *Ita of Killeedy*
Three other women saints figure fairly prominently in the early history of the Church in Ireland: Gobnet, Moninne and Ita.

The first-named belongs to the fifth and early sixth centuries. She
was, therefore, a contemporary of Brigit. Born in Co Clare, she spent
some time in the Aran Islands, then moved to Co Waterford to set
up a church at Kilgobnet, and finally settled at Ballyvourney in Co
Cork where she built a convent. We have very little definite information about her. An enthusiastic apiarist, her symbol is the humble
bee.

Moninne is associated with the convents of Faughart, near the town
of Dundalk, and Killeavy, in what is now south Armagh. The date of
her death is uncertain but we do know that she belonged to the
generation after Brigit.

Ita was an abbess in her native west Limerick and is credited, as 'the
foster-mother of the saints of Ireland', with training a number of
young boys, including Brendan of Clonfert, in the ways of the Faith.
She is sometimes referred to as the 'Brigit of Munster'. Ita died about
570.

Patrick's admiration for his female religious knew no bounds. His exemplary nuns are unnamed, nevertheless, in either of his writings. The fact that we can mention merely four Irish women saints does not mean that nuns were an insignificant minority in Irish society. Their very anonymity is doubtless eloquent testimony to their genuine and effective living-out of their call to Christian perfection. We shall leave the final comment on this topic to the chivalrous Bede, who says in his treatise on the Old Testament books of Esdras: 'Fittingly are men's voices joined with the singing of women, for among women also there are those who, not only by their lives but even by preaching, can set fire to the hearts of others in praise of their Creator, no doubt on account of their feminine nature; as though by the very sweetness of their holy voices they assist in the work of building the temple of the Lord.'

Notes:
1. See Chapter Ten.

2. Clonmacnois was one of the most distinguished of all the Irish monasteries. Its history covers more than a millennium. Donnchadh Ó Floinn's lively prose, penned in 1968, captures its significance, and that of so many similar foundations: 'Maynooth ... is now 173 years of age ... Clonmacnois survived six Maynooth lifetimes. When it was nearly three times as old as Maynooth is now, the Cross of the Scriptures ... was erected to the memory of the King, Flann Sinna. Another Maynooth lifetime passed, and it was producing another work which still survives, the Book of the Dun Cow. When the Normans landed, the monastery was beginning its seventh century: as if Maynooth should witness a strange invasion in the 25th century. After another Maynooth lifetime, Bruce was landing in Carrickfergus. It was in its tenth century when the Gothic doorway of the cathedral there was erected by Dean Odo. And it had passed its thousand years when Henry VIII suppressed it. Oxford will not be as old as Clonmacnois for another hundred years. From the hundreds of references to it in the annals you will see how largely it bulked in the life of Ireland ...'

3. Tim Severin and his shipmates in their Brendan Voyage, during the summers of 1976 and 1977, proved that such an expedition in a sixth-century craft was possible. Severin and his party managed to take their curragh across the Atlantic from Co Kerry via the Hebrides, Faroes, Iceland and Greenland to Peckford Island, in the Outer Wadham Group, some one hundred and fifty miles north-west of St John's, Newfoundland, reaching the New World at 8.00 p.m. on 26th June 1977.

4. See De Paor, Liam, Saint Patrick's World (Blackrock, Co Dublin, 1993).

5. Many double monasteries grew up in Anglo-Saxon England in the seventh century but they did not last long for the Vikings destroyed every one of them and later monasteries were all single.

Colum Cille

*'... there came from Ireland
to Britain a priest and abbot
named Columba, a true monk
in life no less than habit;
he came to Britain
to preach the word of God
to the kingdoms
of the northern Picts
which are separated from
the southern part of their land
by steep and rugged mountains.'*

[Bede's *Ecclesiastical History of the English People*, iii. 4]

Colum Cille, Ireland's first great missionary, is regarded as one of the three patron saints of Ireland. As with Patrick and Brigit, the other two national tutelaries, many of the details of his life are vague or controversial. A limited amount of background information is to be found in the *Amra Choluim Chille* (*A Poem in Praise of Colum Cille*), a eulogy – 'the oldest piece of European vernacular poetry', according to Francis J Byrne – composed on the saint's death by Dallán Forgaill. The Venerable Bede (672-735), in his *Ecclesiastical History*, finished in 731, supplies us with certain details regarding the saint. We can also learn some things about our subject from the *Annals*, and from the *Altus Prosator* (the title of which in English is *Ancient of Days*) and the *Noli Pater* (*Do not, O Father*), poems apparently by Colum Cille himself. All these works, however, contain little solid material on which to build a historical account. For substantial information about Colum Cille our chief source is Adomnan who wrote his *Life of Colum Cille* about a hundred years after the death of the saint.

Adomnan, a descendant of Colum Cille's family, the Cenél Conaill, was born in Co Donegal some thirty years after the death of Colum Cille. He was possibly educated at Clonard (but some scholars view him as a likely alumnus of Durrow) before joining the community at Iona about 650. He became ninth abbot of the Columban mother house in 679. The main literary undertakings of this unique product of the Irish monastic schools, both written in Latin, were the *De Locis Sanctis (Concerning the Holy Places)*, a topographical account of the Holy Land, and the *Life of Columba*. An examination of these works shows that he was an accomplished scholar and worthy of Bede's commendation: 'a wise and good man with an excellent knowledge of the scriptures' [v.15].

Writing sometime between 688 and 704, Adomnan divides his description of 'the life and character of this our Columba' [Second Preface, 3b] into three books. The first deals with prophetic revelations, the second with miracles, and the third with appearances of angels. Clearly, then, historical accuracy and critical evaluation were not for Adomnan of paramount importance. He was not writing a history nor a biography. He was concerned to show through a myriad of miracles, wonders and prophecies the sanctity of his subject. As a result some scholars question the *Life*'s historical worth. The most sceptical dismiss the work altogether. Schoel, for example, has gone so far as to observe that it is 'so obscured by fables that one could scarcely believe that such nonsense could have been written in the seventh century when learning flourished at Iona.' The careful agree with Anderson and Anderson that Adomnan's 'value is less for the history of Columba than for his own ideas, and for the circumstances of his own time.' The confident side with Bishop William Reeves when he evaluates the *Life* as perhaps the most valuable monument of the Irish Church which has escaped the ravages of time. The weight of modern scholarship supports Reeves's position.

A recent book on the subject is Máire Herbert's scholarly *Iona, Kells, and Derry. The History and Hagiography of the Monastic 'Familia' of Columba* (Oxford, 1988). Doctor Herbert uncovers an 'Iona stratum' in the *Life*, what she calls a 'coherent body of narrative', which apparently dates from the early seventh century. This was transmitted to Adomnan by oral tradition and through a now lost written record drawn up during the monastic careers in Scotland of Segéne and his nephew Cumméne, fifth and seventh abbot of Iona respectively. In this monastic stratum 'the background detail is minutely sketched, and ordinary, even trivial, events of community life provide the setting in which the sanctity of Colum Cille is revealed.' And so in the *Life* we find numerous rich details of the day-to-day life of Colum

Cille and his community. We learn of the generous welcome bestowed upon guests [i.4]; of the monks' efforts to bring building-materials by ship to their community [ii.2]; of their construction of dry-stone enclosures [ii.27]; of a redundant mill-stone being used to support a cross [iii.23]; of monks returning to the monastery in the evening after working at the harvest [i.37]; of pigs fattened on the fruit of trees [ii.23]; and so forth. There is in the *Life*, too, as the late Kathleen Hughes has pointed out, a wealth of more significant, if incidental, historical information {Note 1}.

In the *Life* we discover something of the Irish and Scottish princes of Colum Cille's day: King Conall of Dál Riata; King Aedán and his son Eochaid; King Aed Sláine of Brega; King Aed of the Cenél Conaill and his son Domnall. We glean, too, some information about the Brittonic King Roderc of Strathclyde and the Anglean King Oswald of Northumbria. The *Life* also provides us with material relating to Pictland. From it we discover that King Bruide had a subordinate king in the Orkneys; that the northern Picts were largely heathen in Colum Cille's day and that the saint did some missionary work among them; and, dare we say it, that in the sixth century Loch Ness was inhabited by the monster which, fourteen hundred years later, neither historical nor scientific criticism has managed to kill! Although Adomnan was a hagiographer, he was concerned with a truthful portrayal of his subject. The author himself states that he would not write 'either falsehood, or things that might be doubtful or unsure' [Second Preface 3b]. He says that he obtained his oral information from 'trustworthy men who knew the facts' [Second Preface 3b]. And so it is with a certain degree of confidence that we use his opus as our chief source of information about the saint.

Colum Cille was born on 7th December 521 at Gartan, Co Donegal and belonged to the Cenél Conaill, a branch of the Uí Néill dynasty. His father's name was Feidlimid and his grand-father was Conall Gulban after whom the sept was named. Conall Gulban's father is reputed to have been Niall Noígiallach, that half-legendary figure who gave his name to the mighty Uí Néill. Colum Cille's mother was Eithne, a princess from Leinster. He was baptised by Cruithnechan and was initially called Criomhthann, meaning 'fox' – and for all his life he displayed a certain vulpine shrewdness – but was sometime later given the name Colum Cille ('Dove of the Church'). In accordance with the Irish custom of fosterage, the holy man Cruithnechan, an Irish Pict, became the boy's foster-father and commenced his education. Cruithnechan lived near Kilmacrennan, not far from Gartan. From there Colum Cille proceeded to Leinster where, tradition tells us, he was taught by a Christian bard named Gemman.

This possibly accounts for his later close relationship with the *filid*, the Irish poets. Next Colum Cille moved to Clonard to study under Finnian, the most learned teacher of his day and the *magister (teacher)* of the Irish monks.

It was by being ordained a priest, while he was at Clonard, that Colum Cille turned his back on his distinguished lineage which might have led him to the High Kingship of the Uí Néill. By so doing he probably gave monasticism and priesthood respectability for the most significant stratum of society. And a priest he remained for the rest of his days: he never received the fullness of orders by being raised to the episcopate. Tradition has it that Colum Cille completed his education by spending some time in Saint Mobhi's monastery of Glasnevin and that he may have visited Enda of Aran and Finnian of Moville. While in Glasnevin one of his contemporaries was Canice; another may have been Comgall.

According to the *Annals of Ulster* Colum Cille made his first monastic foundation in 546 at Derry when he was aged twenty-five. His other major foundation in Ireland was at Durrow in Co Offaly. Both these settlements would have been located at once-pagan holy places. Although over fifty monasteries in Ireland and Scotland are associated with Colum Cille, it is probable that only three were directly founded by the saint himself. He definitely founded Durrow, though it is more likely, as Alfred P Smyth suggests, that he established it in the final decade of his life than in the 550s as is traditionally held. Smyth's approach is supported by Doctor Herbert.

One would like to believe that Derry owes its existence to him also and that it was his first foundation. Although references to Derry in the *Life* are scant and inconclusive and although some modern scholars {Note 2} are inclined to question Colum Cille's personal identification with it, his association with the place is reverently held and we are happy to accept the reliability of the hallowed tradition which makes Colum Cille its founder. Our confidence in linking the saint with Derry is supported by A D S MacDonald's article in *Peritia* on 'Aspects of the Monastery and Monastic Life in Adomnan's *Life of Columba*'. The Cork archaeologist suggests that references in the *Life* to a woman having sought sanctuary in the church and cemetery 'in the oakwood of Calcach' [i.20] denote the existence of a monastic enclosure there.

As we shall see, Colum Cille most certainly set up Iona. The other houses in the *paruchia Columbae* were most probably established by monks of Colum Cille's community – a few perhaps during his lifetime but most in the decades, and indeed centuries, after his death.

Some of the most notable among these foundations were Kells, Swords, Drumcliffe, Moone and Tory.

Colum Cille served the Church in Ireland for some seventeen years until in 563 he made the decision to go into exile. Probably no other event in his life has caused so much controversy. Adomnan tells us that two years after the battle of Cúl Dreimne Colum Cille went to Iona 'wishing to be a pilgrim for Christ' [Second Preface, 4a]. For centuries, however, others have been more suspicious of the saint's motives. The Scottish historian, W Douglas Simpson, writing in 1927, is of this school. He claims that 'on the day of Pentecost, 13th May 563, the exiled strife-monger, with guilt heavy on his soul and bitterness gnawing at his heart, landed on Iona.' It is Adomnan's method of dating Colum Cille's departure, by using the battle, which has led some to connect the two incidents. At Cúl Dreimne the northern Uí Néill fought with and defeated the forces of Diarmait Mac Cerbaill, the so-called High King, killing three thousand of his warriors. Theories on the origins of the battle differ.

The causes could have been political; they could have been politico-religious; or they could have been personal. Some hold that Colum Cille was the protector of Curnan, son of the king of the Connachta, who was killed by a member of King Diarmait's immediate family and that his guarantor had to avenge his death. Others claim that the saint was angered by the pagan elements still obvious in the *feis* at Tara, held by King Diarmait to inaugurate his reign. Yet others believe the most popular tradition that Colum Cille surreptitiously copied a scriptural text in the possession of Finnian of Moville; that Finnian claimed exclusive rights to the book; that the arbitrator Diarmait judged in favour of Finnian with the remark, 'to every cow her calf, to every book its copy'; and that the battle of Cúl Dreimne was the result of Colum Cille's thirst for revenge. Though there is only slender evidence for this theory in the authentic sources (Alfred P. Smyth, for example, mentions a scar on the saint's corpse as possibly indicating a warfaring past), Colum Cille certainly does seem to have had an interest in the battle and its results. This is hardly surprising for his was an intensely political background. The *Annals of Ulster* tell us that it was 'through the prayers of Colum Cille' that victory was achieved for the northern Uí Néill. This interest, active or intercessionary, seems to have been discussed at a synod in Teltown (c 562) where an earlier decision to excommunicate Colum Cille was revoked.

Adomnan does make passing reference to this incident but again gives no indication that it was related to Colum Cille's resolution to leave Ireland. In the years to follow many monks were to take his example in their endeavour to follow Christ. It is almost inconceivable that they would have followed 'the way of Colum Cille' if the origins of his missionary exile were to be traced to crime and an imposed penance. And so it is more probable that in May 563 Colum Cille with twelve disciples set sail from Ireland for the noblest of motives: that of going into 'exile for the love of Christ'.

They sailed to Iona, a small island at the tip of Mull off the west coast of Scotland which is about eighty miles from the Co Antrim coast and is invisible from Ireland. South-east of Iona on the mainland was the Scottic territory of Dál Riata, an extension of that sept's domain in north-eastern Ireland, and to their north was the kingdom of the Picts. Three years before the arrival of Colum Cille the Picts had gone to war with the Scots and had defeated them, thereby reducing their power in Scotland. This was the state of affairs when Colum Cille arrived.

Colum Cille was to work on Iona for the remaining thirty-four years of his life. Founding a monastic settlement, he built up a large community on the island. He devoted himself to prayer, study and physical work. Over the centuries, Iona was certainly a place of great learning and craftmanship, producing works like *Concerning the Holy Places* and the *Life of Columba* and (probably) the now-lost *Iona Chronicle*, the *Cathach* and the magnificent *Book of Kells*. Indeed, Colum Cille himself may have been responsible for penning the *Cathach*, a copy of the psalms and Ireland's oldest extant manuscript.

The saint also engaged in evangelisation. Unfortunately, the extent and results of that work form but another obscure area of Colum Cille's life. He has been credited with travelling the length and breadth of Scotland converting the heathen Picts and there are numerous ancient church dedications to him which seem to bear this out. Some, mainly Scottish, twentieth-century scholars disagree with the 'orthodox' assessment of the saint's missionary achievements and it would appear that the traditional estimate of his successes is exaggerated. W Douglas Simpson, for instance, would dispute the notion that the Picts were entirely pagan at the time of Colum Cille's arrival. He is of the opinion that predecessors and contemporaries of Colum Cille, such as Ninnian, Kentigern, Comgall, Canice, Moluag, Blaan, Cormac Ua Liathain, Donnan and Finbarr, were responsible for the conversion of many areas of Pictland. Simpson believes that Colum Cille's foundations were almost entirely restricted to the friendly area of Dál Riata and when this kingdom's political influence was extended so, too, was the name of the saint. Though

Simpson is hypercritical, he provides a valuable counter-balance to the traditional approach.

Colum Cille's main work of evangelisation was doubtless done in or around Dál Riata. It was not confined, however, to that region. His name is strongly associated with Loch Ness, the district of Strathtay, Ardnamurchan, and the island of Skye. Adomnan informs us that he needed an interpreter to make himself understood among the Picts. He had, therefore, some significant dealings with them. Bede confirms us in this conclusion when he states that Colum Cille 'came to Britain to preach the word of God to the kingdoms of the northern [as distinct from the southern] Picts'. We know, too, that shortly after arriving at Iona he set out to meet the ruler of the northern Picts, King Bruide. Travelling through the Great Glen, his journey to Bruide's capital at Inverness in the north-east of Scotland was undoubtedly politically as well as religiously motivated. Colum Cille would have been shrewdly aware that, unless his fellow countrymen in Dál Riata were assured of political stability, his missionary successes would have been limited. When they did meet, the saint made a remarkable impression on Bruide though this did not bring about the powerful king's conversion. But the visit did result in the confirmation of Colum Cille's tenure of Iona; it relaxed relations between the Picts and the Scots of Dál Riata; and it ensured that future missionary work among the northern Picts would be a safer task. Even on the remote island of Iona, then, Colum Cille could not distance himself from the political manoeuverings of his day.

His political involvement and his concern for his fellow countrymen in a foreign land are again in evidence when, with the death of King Conall in 574, Colum Cille played a more direct role in the affairs of state of Dál Riata. Eógan, Gabhrán's eldest son, was the more obvious heir but Colum Cille, claiming to have been instructed by an angel, consecrated Gabhrán's youngest son, Aedán, as king instead. This began the tradition of having Scottish kings crowned on the Black Stone of Iona {Note 3}. Although Colum Cille's action was unpopular and the succession of Aedán provoked civil strife amongst the Scots, his protégé proved to be a capable and astute leader. Under his direction the kingdom of Dál Riata was extended at the expense of both the Picts and the Britons.

Colum Cille's last major politico-religious involvement was at a convention, held in 575, at Druim Cett near Limavady, Co. Derry. We need no longer view this as an assembly of all the kings of Ireland accompanied by their advisers, both lay and clerical. The convention was essentially a meeting between Aed, king of Cenél Conaill and perhaps over-king of the northern Uí Néill, and Aedán, king of Dál Riata. John Bannerman has shown that 'the two sections of the Dál Riata, the one in Scotland and the other in Ireland, remained united', under a single king resident in Argyll, until the battle of Mag Roth in 637 after which 'the Scottish and Irish Dál Riatas began to go their separate ways.' Colum Cille's return to Ireland on this particular occasion was not an isolated event; Adomnan states that he made a number of such journeys (hardly, we might add, the behaviour of an exiled miscreant).

The most important civil leader present at Druim Cett was Aed, son of Ainmere, the so-called High King of Ireland. He was anxious to limit the power of the Irish Dál Riata while Colum Cille's chief concern was to look after the interests of the part of Dál Riata in Scotland. The saint negotiated a compromise. Aed was guaranteed the use of the armed forces of Dál Riata in Ireland in time of war, while Aedán's right to levy taxes and tributes in the Irish part of his kingdom was acknowledged.

Colum Cille next sought the liberation of Scandlán, son of Colmán, king of Ossory, who was being held hostage by Aed and was being ill-treated by him. Although apparently unsuccessful on the occasion of Druim Cett, Colum Cille's intervention seems ultimately to have brought about Scandlán's release.

The third important issue at the convention was the position of the *filid*. They were a learned and skilled class of chroniclers who could relate lore and legend in story and verse. The traditional account of this particular controversy is that their numbers had over the decades grown large, some had begun to abuse their privileges and perhaps some were thorns in the flesh of the Establishment. At any rate, the story has it, their opponents presented them in 575 as being little better than venomous beggars and a proposal was made to expel them all from Ireland. Colum Cille, himself a trained poet, defended them, highlighting the wealth of learning that would be lost should their order be exiled. As a result of the case he made for the bards, a compromise was reached: the poets would be allowed to remain in the country but their numbers were to be reduced and their privileges curbed. There is, doubtless, a kernel of truth in this traditional account. The more likely scenario, however, is that the ancient priestly caste of the *filid* had been superseded by the Christian Church and that, at Druim Cett, Colum Cille found the poets a new and respected, but subordinate and benign, place in sixth-century Irish society.

From what has been said above it is obvious that Colum Cille was a canny politician who involved himself deeply in the affairs of his day. But he was no mere politician. He was above all a man of outstanding sanctity. Daphne D C Pochin Mould has demonstrated that he emerges from the *Life* as a kindly individual with a genuine interest in and practical concern for people. He helped the unfortunate: curing a nun with a broken hip [ii.5], rehabilitating a reformed robber [i.41], assisting a woman in the pangs of child-birth with his prayers [ii.40], providing destitute men with the means of feeding themselves [ii.37], and even as his death approached in June 597 {Note 4} comforting others rather than seeking to be comforted [iii.23]. He had a profound sense of the worth of human beings and of the contribution they were making to society. He saw meaning in every life lived to the full, no matter how seemingly unimportant, as was the case with the smith, Colum Coilrigin [iii.9]. Like so many other Irish saints, he was in harmony with nature: for instance, the old monastery pony could mourn his approaching death [iii.23] and he revived a crane which had been driven onto the beach at Iona in a storm [i.48].

Our Lord has invited us all to 'be wily as serpents and as innocent as doves'. Like all intelligent followers of Christ, Colum Cille could see through hypocrites and never countenanced evil nor tolerated evildoers but invariably welcomed and reconciled the truly repentant. And so we find him castigating evildoers [see i.21 and ii. 22-25, for instance] and yet welcoming the sincerely contrite like Libran [ii.39]. Above all Colum Cille was a man of prayer. Adomnan tells us how central the Divine Office [i.37] and the Mass [see i.40 and iii.23, for example] were to the saint's life and suggests that liturgical prayer fed his spiritual life and occasionally allowed him to experience ecstasy in mystical contemplation [see iii.18, for example]. Some writers have dismissed Colum Cille as a pragmatist and a politician. This is unfair. Coming as he did from a princely background and having a commanding and practical personality, he was bound to make an enormous impact on the life and affairs of his generation. His real greatness, however, was that he was able to combine the advantages given him by temperament and birth with the ambition of sainthood.

In fact Colum Cille was our first great native saint. In one sense he was a consolidator, for by his complete identification with the Church he managed to integrate it into Celtic society. In another sense he was a pioneer, the original Irish 'pilgrim for Christ'. He inspired monks from Iona to evangelise Northumbria, and thence indirectly many other parts of England, and monks from Ireland – Columban, for example – to carry the Gospel to the continent.

Notes:

1. In Adomnan we read that the Scots of Dál Riata participated in the important battle of Mag Roth (Moira) in Co Down, one of the significant stepping-stones in the advance of the northern Uí Néill in Ulster. This battle took place in 637. The 'incidental historical information' can refer to events of Colum Cille's own time or to happenings in the period between the saint's death and the completion of the *Life* by the author.

2. Anderson and Anderson, for example, see the monastery of Derry as definitely a part of the celebrated *paruchia Columbae* but not as one of the saint's own foundations. This is a view also taken by Brian Lacey in his recent *Siege City: The Story of Derry and Londonderry* (Belfast, 1990).

3. This stone is still part of the ceremonial chair used at the coronation of a modern British monarch.

4. Colum Cille's feast-day is still widely celebrated in Ireland on the 9th June each year. It is remembered particularly in Derry where many people wear oak-leaves in their lapels in his honour.

CHAPTER EIGHT

Prominent Irish Saints in Britain

'...Entrusting himself
to the holy company
of the eternal God,
and following the divine command,
he sailed in the ship
that was awaiting him
... to Britain.'

[Muirchú]

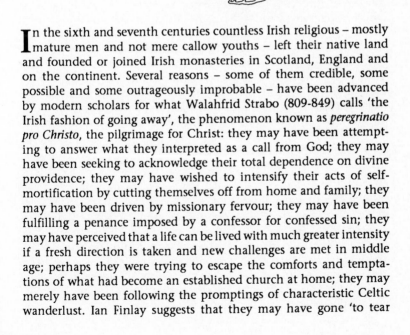

In the sixth and seventh centuries countless Irish religious – mostly mature men and not mere callow youths – left their native land and founded or joined Irish monasteries in Scotland, England and on the continent. Several reasons – some of them credible, some possible and some outrageously improbable – have been advanced by modern scholars for what Walahfrid Strabo (809-849) calls 'the Irish fashion of going away', the phenomenon known as *peregrinatio pro Christo*, the pilgrimage for Christ: they may have been attempting to answer what they interpreted as a call from God; they may have been seeking to acknowledge their total dependence on divine providence; they may have wished to intensify their acts of self-mortification by cutting themselves off from home and family; they may have been driven by missionary fervour; they may have been fulfilling a penance imposed by a confessor for confessed sin; they may have perceived that a life can be lived with much greater intensity if a fresh direction is taken and new challenges are met in middle age; perhaps they were trying to escape the comforts and temptations of what had become an established church at home; they may merely have been following the promptings of characteristic Celtic wanderlust. Ian Finlay suggests that they may have gone 'to tear

83

themselves free of those pagan roots which are so constantly showing themselves' in the early Irish Church. This seems unlikely as
they were going to lands which were much more pagan than the
country from which they were escaping. Dom Henri Leclercq's fanciful
theory that they were fraudulent, sun-seeking gourmands – primitive versions of our trippers to the Costa del Sol – deserves to be
mentioned merely to be dismissed.

Essentially, Colum Cille pioneered the movement by going to Iona
in 563 and using it as a base from which to consolidate Christianity
in Dál Riata and Pictland {Note 1}. Tradition associates him with
several places in the territories of the Scots and the Picts. Some of
these links with specific localities were doubtless forged by the saint
himself. Others may, however, merely reveal something of the extent of the *paruchia Columbae* built up by monks from Iona like
Donnan, the founder of the monastery of Eigg who was martyred
along with his fifty-two brethren in 618, and Machar, who evangelised
Mull and then Aberdeenshire in later decades. Yet others may give
evidence of a flourishing but relatively late cult of Colum Cille in
Scotland. Despite the wealth of associations, it must be pointed out
that Colum Cille was not the only evangelist to work in what is now
Scotland during our period.

A brief description of the political geography of early medieval Scotland will help us consider the contribution of some of these others
to the spread of the faith in that country. In the sixth century,
northern Britain was occupied by four distinct races. To the extreme
north and north-east were the Picts. To the west, in what is now
known after them as Argyll and in the islands off its coast, with
their capital at Dunadd, were the Scots of Dál Riata, thrusting *emigrés*
from Ireland. To the east and south-east, in the northern part of the
kingdom of Northumbria, with their king residing at Bamburgh,
were the pagan Angles, a Teutonic tribe who had only recently arrived from Scandinavia. And in the south and south-west were the
Britons, Celts whose king had his palace at Dumbarton ('the fort of
the Britons').

Of these four peoples only the Angles were totally pagan. The Scots
of Dál Riata were as Christian as their kinsmen across the North
Channel. The Britons already had a fairly rich Christian heritage,
having been converted by Ninian, who had also done a certain
amount of missionary work among the southern Picts. Ninian's
efforts were continued, from his monastery of *Candida Casa*, by
monks like Kentigern, the celebrated Brittonic founder of the
church of Glasgow, and by monks from monasteries, which alumni

of Whithorn had established, like Banchory set up by Ternan and Drostan's foundation of Deer. Comgall, Mirin, Moluag, Cathan, Baithene and Blaan, notable contemporaries of Colum Cille who laboured in Scotland, were all products of Bangor, the venerable monastery of the Irish Picts: similarily Maelrubha, founder of the important monastery of Applecross, who was perhaps the most famous of all. Although Maelrubha was a member of the Cenél nEógain (part of the Uí Néill) on his father's side, his mother was of the Cruithne (the Irish Picts). In the last quarter of the seventh century and up until his death in 722, he worked indefatigably in Pictland, evangelising Skye and the Scottish mainland as far north as Loch Broom.

Another Irishman of the same ethnic background who ministered in Pictland was Colum Cille's devoted friend Canice. One of Canice's disciples at his monastery of Rigmond (or St Andrew's) was Riaghail. Other Irish monks who worked independently of Colum Cille as evangelists in Scotland were: Finnian of Moville, Brendan of Clonfert, Cormac Ua Liathain, Findbarr of Cork, who gave his name to the island of Barra, and Flannan, after whom some of the islands of the Hebrides, to the west of Lewis and Harris, are named. There is a germ of truth in W Douglas Simpson's [1927] observation that, 'the Pictish Church was based upon three main centres, *Candida Casa* and Glasgow, both of the Britons, and Bangor of the Irish Picts; and none of these had any organic connection whatsoever with Iona.'

It was from Iona, however, that the Irish missionaries made the most significant contribution to the expansion of Christianity in the island of Britain for it was monks from Colum Cille's foundation who converted the pagan inhabitants of Northumbria, the Angles. These recent colonists from Scandinavia, together with the Jutes and the Saxons, had invaded and subjugated Britain in the fifth century. The Jutes settled in Kent where they set up a small but influential kingdom. The Saxons occupied much of the south of the country, founding three kingdoms: Essex, Sussex and Wessex. The Angles took control of most of the territory extending from the Thames to Edinburgh. They established three distinct kingdoms: East Anglia, Mercia and Northumbria. This last-mentioned kingdom (the 'North-Humber-land') was the most powerful of all the Anglo-Saxon nations. It stretched from the Humber and the Mersey to the Firth of Forth. At times during its chequered history it was divided into two princi-palities; Bernicia in the north and Deira in the south.

The conversion of the Anglo-Saxons is a remarkable story. It was accomplished by two independent groups: Roman missionaries and

Irish *peregrini*. By the time Augustine of Canterbury died in 605, Kent and Essex had been 'converted' by the Romans, but their allegiance to Christianity was dependent on the goodwill of the kings, and by 616 – with the deaths of the convert kings of Kent and Essex and their replacement by pagan successors – the Jutes and the East-Saxons had reverted to paganism. Similarly in Northumbria, the overthrow of the Christian King Edwin by Caedwalla and Penda saw that kingdom relapse into paganism. Edwin had been won over to Christianity by his new wife Aethelburh and her chaplain Bishop Paulinus, one of the second group of monks sent by Saint Gregory from Rome in 601. The Roman missionaries aimed at mass conversions rather than truly solid ones and so their labours were shallow and transient rather than transforming and lasting.

In 634, in the Battle of Hefenfelth, near Hexham, control of Northumbria was gained by Oswald, one of the sons of Aethelfrith, a former King of Northumbria. Oswald had spent the whole reign of Edwin, his father's rival and successor, in exile with his brothers, as Bede tells us, 'among the Irish or the Picts' (iii.1). Bede states further that he had been 'instructed in the Faith as the Irish taught it ... and regenerated by the grace of baptism' (iii.1). Enriched by a culture other and older than his own, Oswald invited the abbot of Iona to send missionaries to his kingdom. Corman, an Iona monk, accepted the challenge but did not persevere. He was replaced by Aidan, another monk of Iona, who had been educated at Senan's monastery on Scattery Island in the estuary of the Shannon, and had possibly been at one time the bishop of Clogher.

Aidan arrived in Northumbria in 635, establishing himself on Lindisfarne, an island just off the coast near Bamburgh, the Northumbrian royal residence. This spot is sometimes referred to as the 'Holy Island'. It was to become a most powerful centre of religious influence in England. Bede tells us that Aidan's co-workers were two Irishmen but unhappily does not give us their names or any details about them. Bede is our chief source of information about Aidan. He is quite a reliable source for he was born less than a quarter of a century after the great saint's death and was a historian with scrupulous scholarly standards. Despite his strong disapproval of Aidan's adherence to Celtic usages regarding the dating of Easter, for example, Bede gives us a warm and loving description of the saint's character. He calls him a person of the greatest compassion, piety, moderation and consistency. He speaks admiringly of Aidan's dedication to the virtue of poverty and of his love for the poor. He stresses that the abbot, while being a most approachable and friendly person, who stopped to talk to everyone whom he met on his travels, was nevertheless a most careful and contemplative man. Bede emphasises that one of Aidan's priorities was to train a native clergy and that he chose twelve Anglo-Saxon youths for this purpose. Aidan's missionary policy was, then, akin to Patrick's.

Like Patrick, too, he had a special interest in the redemption of slaves. Oswald gave Aidan invaluable assistance, adding weight to his evangelisation by acting as his interpreter and always giving him his support. Aidan founded churches, oratories and monasteries – for instance, Melrose, the first abbot of which was Eata, one of his twelve Anglo-Saxon pupils, and the double monasteries of Hartlepool, Coldingham and Tadcaster – in every part of the kingdom. The first abbess of Coldingham was Saint Aebbe, King Oswald's sister. In 642 Oswald died in the Battle of Maserfelth against Penda, the pagan King of Mercia. His corpse was dismembered and offered to Woden on the victor's orders. The Northumbrian King's sacrificial death, following his dedicated Christian life, has caused him to be venerated as a saint. He was succeeded by Oswiu, who got the principality of Bernicia, and Oswine, who took control of Deira. The latter became Aidan's protégé. He was murdered by his cousin and rival Oswiu in 651 and the apostle of Northumbria died twelve days later on 31st August.

Finan was chosen as Aidan's successor. An Irishman and a member of the community at Iona, he erected a cathedral at Lindisfarne 'after the Irish method', as Bede records, in one of the earliest descriptions of an Irish church, 'not of stone but of hewn oak, thatching it with reeds' [iii.25]. He sent missions to Mercia and Essex when Northumbria became predominant in England. Under the guidance of Finan, Oswiu made amends for Oswine's murder by founding the monasteries of Gilling and Tynemouth. He also established the double monastery of Whitby, making Hilda its first abbess, in gratitude to God for routing Penda in battle. Hilda had taken over the government of the monastery of Hartlepool in 649 from its first abbess Heiu, who had gone to govern the double monastery of Tadcaster. After Hilda's death in 680, Whitby was governed by Oswiu's daughter, Aelfflaed, and her mother, Eanflaed, ruling in tandem. Whitby was the sepulchre of the Northumbrian royal family. Here, too, the monk-poet Caedmon, one of the earliest identifiable bards in the Old English language, lies buried. It was at Whitby that the famous Synod was held in 664, three years after Finan's death, during the rule of the abbot Colmán. This assembly ruled in favour of Roman practices, in preference to Irish usages, regarding the dating of Easter and other matters. The chief advocate of Celtic practices at the Synod of Whitby, Colmán, resigned his see when Oswiu decided against him and went via Iona to the west of Ireland to found the monasteries of Inishbofin, for his Irish monks, and Mayo, for his English brethren. Colmán died at Inishbofin in 676.

The influence of the Irish Church in Northumbria, however, did not end with the withdrawal of Colmán. Another Irish bishop, Tuda, was appointed to succeed him. A Munsterman, he had taken the Roman side in the paschal controversy. His appointment was doubtless an attempt to unite the Roman and Irish factions in Northumbria. But his episcopate lasted only a few months, for he was carried off in the Yellow Plague later in 664 {Note 2}. Eata, the abbot of Melrose, one of the twelve Anglians trained by Aidan and a firm advocate of Celtic practices at the Synod of Whitby, was next appointed to the see.

He had for his successor Cuthbert, who was ordained bishop of Lindisfarne in 684. Some writers – Cardinal Moran and Mary Ryan D'Arcy, for instance – are convinced that Cuthbert was born in Ireland. It is safer to view him, nevertheless, with Alfred P Smyth, as an Englishman 'who in the heroic sanctity of his life combined all that was best in the traditions of early Celtic and Anglo-Saxon Christianity.' Influenced greatly in his youth by Boisil, a monk who had himself been formed in the Irish monastic tradition, he entered Melrose in 651 but later moved to the abortive foundation of Ripon with the abbot Eata, future bishop of Lindisfarne. He was at different times prior of Melrose and Lindisfarne. After the Synod of Whitby he adopted Roman customs and by patient persistence slowly won over the monks to his point of view. Although Cuthbert was trained in the Irish tradition, he should be viewed as a moderate figure – someone who healed the wounds left by the paschal controversy. Even on his death-bed, more than a score of years after the Synod of Whitby, he warned his brethren against the danger of schism, advising them, as Bede records in his *Life of Cuthbert*, to avoid dealings 'with those who had wandered from the unity of the Church either through not celebrating Easter at the proper time or through evil living' [Chapter 39]. He was known for his asceticism, preaching, and scrupulous visitation of his diocese. He died in 687 at the age of fifty-three.

Even with the death of Cuthbert the Irish Church continued for some time to have an influence in Northumbria. Its next three bishops – Eadberht, Eadfrith and Aethelwold – were all steeped in the traditions of the Celtic Church. Above all, perhaps, its poet-king Aldfrith, the son of an Uí Néill princess and Adomnan's past-pupil and friend, ensured that Irish influences continued in the territory. Eadfrith was one of the most notable of the bishops of Lindisfarne. He

Celtic Monastic Sites,
Political Centres
and Major Kingdoms
of Scotland, Wales and England
in the Seventh Century

Skye
Applecross
Eigg

Northern Picts

Inverness
Banchory
Deer

Iona
Dunadd

Dal Riata

Southern Picts

St Andrew's

Edinburgh

Dumbarton
Glasgow

Coldingham
Lindisfarne
Bamburgh

Melrose

Bernicia

Northern
Britons

Carlisle

Northumbria

Tynemouth
Jarrow
Wearmouth
Hartlepool
Whitby

Whithorn
(Candida Casa)

Gilling

Deira

Lastingham
Ripon

Tadcaster

Anglesea

Mercia
Lichfield

East Anglia

Peterborough

Burgh Castle

St David's (Mynwy)

Essex

Caldey Island

Malmesbury

Tilbury
London
Canterbury

Bradwell-on-Sea

Glastonbury
Sherborne

Wessex

Sussex

Bosham

Kent

was educated in Ireland and was a first-class scholar and calligrapher. It seems almost certain that he penned the renowned Lindisfarne Gospels, a manuscript which displays the marriage of the Irish and Roman elements in Northumbria within a generation of the Synod of Whitby. Aethelwold was the last 'Irish' bishop of Lindisfarne. He died in 640. Thereafter Irish influence in Northumbria decreased and a few decades later, with the incursions of the Vikings, the Celtic twilight in northern England gave way to darkness.

In conclusion, we note the religious influence, particularly during the episcopate of Finan, exercised by Northumbria and its Celtic missionaries and by Irish *peregrini* coming directly from Ireland, on the other Anglo-Saxon kingdoms of Mercia, Essex, East Anglia, Sussex and Wessex.

According to Bede, in 652 Peada, Penda's son, was baptised by Finan, 'together with all the *gesiths* and *thegns* who had come with him' [iii.21], in order to marry Oswiu's daughter, Alhflaed. When he ascended the throne of Mercia on his father's violent death in 654, Peada invited an Irishman called Diuma and three other priests, all from Lindisfarne, to evangelise his kingdom and to establish a monastery at Peterborough. After Peada's death Oswiu assumed control of Mercia and had Diuma ordained bishop. Diuma died in 658. He was succeeded in turn by two Irishmen, Cellach and Jaruman, and two Englishmen trained by the Irish. By the time the last of these, Chad – one of Aidan's twelve Anglo-Saxon pupils – died, in 672, Mercia was fairly solidly Christian and the foundations of the see of Lichfield had been laid. We must never, however, exaggerate successes in mission territories. It takes Christianity several decades to penetrate fully hearts and minds. In Mercia, for example, Peada was murdered at Easter 654 by the treachery of the woman for whom he had originally adopted the faith: the temporary triumph of politics and the Prince of this World over piety and the Prince of Peace.

Sigeberht, the King of Essex, was converted in 653 due to the influence of Oswiu and requested that missionaries be sent. Finan sent Cedd, another of Aidan's English pupils and Chad's brother, to evangelise the kingdom. He set up monasteries at Bradwell-on-Sea and Tilbury, both of which were based on the Lindisfarne model. Cedd also founded the monastery of Lastingham in Yorkshire. Cedd was present at the Synod of Whitby. On his death later in 664, the Irishman Jaruman, one of Diuma's successors in Mercia, went to work among the East Saxons.

A different Sigeberht was King of the East Angles in the middle decades of the seventh century. He ascended the throne in 631. He had been baptised in his youth while exiled in Gaul. He christianised his country with the help of a French bishop, Felix, and with the assistance of the Irish abbot Fursa who came directly from Ireland to East Anglia in 633, accompanied by his brothers Foillan and Ultán. Fursa erected a monastery at Cnobheresburg, now Burgh Castle, near Great Yarmouth in Suffolk. He laboured for more than twelve years there before proceeding to the continent on the death of Sigeberht in battle against Penda, King of Mercia. His work in England was continued by his brothers until they, too, departed for France.

One of Fursa's companions, a monk named Dicul, was the first evangelist to minister to the South Saxons. He founded the monastery of Bosham at what is now known as Chichester. His work was continued by Wilfrid, an English product of Lindisfarne, the great pro-Roman at the Synod of Whitby and ultimately bishop of York. Wilfrid was known for his pragmatism.

Glastonbury, one of the most famous of the ancient monasteries of Great Britain, is in modern-day Somerset. It was probably not included in the kingdom of Wessex before 721. Until then, Glastonbury was most likely in territory still inhabited by the native Britons. Without any doubt, however, it had Irish connections from a very early date. It was known as 'Glastonbury of the Irish'. Tradition links it with Saint Patrick and some scholars even identify it with the elusive *Bannavem Taberniae*. The relics of 'Old Patrick', upon whose existence the so-called 'Two Patricks Theory' in part depends, were supposed to be buried there; so, too, the remains of Indract and his nine companions – Irish monks martyred in England in the seventh century.

In the tenth century King Edmund presented Glastonbury with the supposed relics of Saint Hilda, desecrated at the assault by the Vikings on Whitby. Glastonbury's history shows, at the very least, Irish associations with the West Country from a very early date. Wessex itself was evangelised by a Roman missionary called Birinus. He baptised Cynegisl, the King of Wessex who had been converted by his son-in-law, Oswald of Northumbria. Birinus was bishop of Dorchester from 635-650. He established a church at Winchester. His initial work was supplemented by the Frenchman Agilbert who had been inspired by the disciples of Columban and educated in Ireland. He was bishop of Dorchester for at least ten years from his arrival in England in 650. Agilbert featured prominently as a Romanus at the Synod of Whitby. From 668-690 he was bishop of Paris. In Wessex, Agilbert was assisted by an Irish monk, Maeldubh, founder of the monastery of Malmesbury. Aldhelm was the most illustrious of

Maeldubh's pupils. A member of the royal house of Wessex, Aldhelm became abbot of Malmesbury in 675 and in 705 was appointed the first bishop of Sherborne. He is remembered as one of the earliest poets in Old English and for his many treatises in Latin. He died in 709.

It has sometimes been claimed that half of Europe was converted by religious who lived the contemplative life. Christian Britain, at any rate, owes an enormous debt to Irish monk-missionaries. These men were monks first and missionaries afterwards. Through contemplation, liturgy and other good works the coenobite offers an example of true Christian life, that is of the reality of Christ living in the Christian heart. The paradox of missiology is that where monasticism – based on solitude, detachment and meditation – flourishes there the Good News spreads. Wherever a monastery is founded in virgin soil, it becomes the first christian community of a new province acquired for the Kingdom of God. This is being proved true to-day in Calcutta and Addis Ababa. It was equally true of sixth- and seventh-century Britain. And having handed on the faith to their neophytes, the Irish *peregrini*, all of them coenobites, directed their steps to other lands.

Notes:

1. A few obscure monks may have gone forth before Colum Cille.

2. This plague struck the southern shores of England in May 664. A particularly virulent virus, it killed those who caught it within a day. Whole towns and hamlets were decimated. By the winter of the same year it had spread as far as Northumbria. It remained a killer-disease for some twenty years before people became immune.

CHAPTER NINE

Columban and Other Peregrini

*'Providential opportunities
for those who wish
to take the high road
to the topmost peaks of heaven ...'*

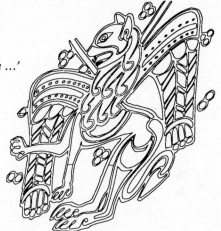

[Columban's *Community Rule*]

Of all the Irish personages of our period none is more accessible than Columban (or Columbanus). This is because we have inherited a vast corpus of his own writings; readily available in G S M Walker's magisterial *Sancti Columbani Opera* (Dublin, 1957) and in Cardinal Ó Fiaich's popular and most readable *Columbanus in his own words* (Dublin, 1974). These sources give us an invaluable insight into the life, character, scholarship, background and convictions of the man. We are also fortunate to have a very early and comparatively reliable *Life* of the saint, Jonas's *Vita*.

Columban was a prolific writer. Happily, although many of his works have perished, many have survived – a rich legacy. The saint produced several different types of writings: letters, sermons, rules, poems and a penitential. Because of its subsequent influence, Columban's *Penitential* is undoubtedly the most significant of his extant writings. His penitential writing was innovative for it brought a system which had been developed in Ireland to the continent and made a major impact on the practice of the discipline of penance there and remotely influenced the evolution of the sciences of moral theology and canon law in the universal Church. His *Regula Monachorum* (*Monks' Rule*) and *Regula Coenobialis* (*Community Rule*), both of which originated in the austerity of Bangor, helped to establish Irish monasticism in western Europe and have contributed to the constitutions of strict religious orders like the Cistercians as we know them to-day. Six of Columban's letters survive. The first of these epistles, dating it seems from 600, was addressed to Pope Gregory the Great. The second was sent to the French bishops assembled at Chalon in 603. The third was to a Pope-Elect and dates from either 604 or 607. The fourth, a warm and affectionate document, was written to his monks remaining in Luxeuil in 610. The fifth, probably also composed in 610, offered encouragement and direction to a young disciple. The sixth rapped the knuckles of Pope Boniface IV in 613. G S M Walker is of the opinion that thirteen of the saint's sermons also survive. This attribution has been challenged but Walker argues convincingly that it is possible to identify Columban's style in these homilies and links them to his sojourn in Milan early in the second decade of the seventh century. The same author also attributes five poems – *The Song on the World's Impermanence, Columbanus to Hunaldus, Saint Columban to Sethus, The Boating Song* and *Columbanus to his Brother Fidolius* – to the pen of the saint.

Jonas's *Life* is a classic example of the hagiographical genre. Its author was born in the small Piedmontese town of Susa, in the foothills of the Italian Alps, close to the modern French border. Jonas was eminently qualified to act as Columban's biographer. He had entered the saint's foundation of Bobbio in 618, three short years after the demise of his subject. There he undoubtedly became acquainted with the personal friends and associates of Columban. From early in his career he acted as secretary to Columban's successors at Bobbio – Attala (615-c 626) and Bertulf (c 626-640). It follows from this fact that he was recognised as being a competent amanuensis and fit for the task of writing the definitive *Life of Columban*. On an investigative mission to France, Jonas also met Eustasius (d 629), abbot of Luxeuil, who had been a disciple of the saint. And one of the author's most enlightening sources was Gall (d 646), Columban's companion for many long years.

Jonas was appointed by Bertulf to compile a *Life* of the saint. He combined the information and insights which he had gained from Columban's associates with material he extracted from the written sources at his disposal, to write the *Life* which he published in 643. Jonas was a conscientious author and hypersensitive to criticism. As a result his book is one of the most reliable histories of its period. However, hagiography will always have its limitations and that of Jonas is no exception: his Latin is excessively flowery; his chronology is somewhat defective; his miracle stories are far-fetched even for the genre; and he never criticises his subject or any of his actions but rather omits episodes that might have reflected badly upon Columban. Nevertheless, Jonas's *Life* is in many ways a coherent, credible and reliable portrayal of the actions and sanctity of a great human being and an invaluable supplement to the extant works of Columban himself.

What, then, do our sources reveal about the career, character and convictions of the founder of Annegray, Luxeuil, Fontaines, Bregenz and Bobbio? Columban was born about 543 into a Christian home in Leinster. His parents were probably of relatively low degree for no hint is given that his were royal or noble antecedents; if he had been of aristocratic parentage the fact would undoubtedly have been mentioned. It would seem that he received some early schooling – in grammar, rhetoric and the scriptures – from a priest in the neighbourhood. A personable youth, in his teens he earned the unwanted attention of some local girls, whom Jonas calls *lascivae puellae* ('lascivious wenches'). This caused him to seek and take the advice of a wise nun. He then turned his back on the temptations offered by this world by embracing the monastic life, despite the vehement protestations of his mother. It is interesting to note, with T M Charles-Edwards, that Jonas describes Columban's anchoretical mentor as having been an exile for fifteen years from her home in her 'place of pilgrimage', evidence that Christians in the Irish tradition made a distinction between two grades of *peregrinatio* – lesser exile at home in the island of Ireland and superior exile abroad. Columban himself was to experience both types of pilgrimage during his long life.

Columban went first to Cleenish on Upper Lough Erne and the school of Saint Sinell who was himself a disciple of Saint Finnian of Clonard. Some scholars identify Sinell with Sillan, third abbot of Bangor. Jonas merely states that Sinell was head of a school of biblical learning. This does not exclude the identification suggested above, for Sinell may later have joined the community at Bangor, or Cleenish may have been a monastery subject to Comgall. Columban was obviously one of Sinell's best pupils for it was while he was in Fermanagh that he wrote a *Commentary on the Psalter* (now lost) and possibly composed his famous poem *The Song on the World's Impermanence*.

After some time – Jonas does not tell us how long – Columban made the decision to move on from Cleenish and join Comgall at Bangor, one of the most austere and scholastic monasteries of his day. Perhaps this was an automatic progression from a daughter monastery to the mother house. We can say with certainty, however, that Columban was already intentionally fostering in himself the characteristics of asceticism and scholarship which were to be the hallmarks of the man. At Bangor the monk Columban was ordained a priest. He spent some thirty years under Comgall, acting for much of this time as the senior lecturer in the monastic school. In his middle years he decided in his determined way to redirect the course of his life by changing from 'lesser exile' in an Irish monastery to 'superior pilgrimage' abroad. He obtained the permission of a reluctant Comgall and in 591 set out with twelve companions for France. Of the twelve, Gall is the most renowned. The names of some of the others in Columban's retinue have also been preserved: Domoal, Comininus, Eunocus, Equonanus, Deicolus, Columban the Younger, Libranus and Aed.

When Columban arrived in France, Roman Gaul no longer existed and the Merovingians were in power. Gaul in the fifth century was still a Roman province but its days as such were numbered. Already barbarian invaders had breached its frontiers; in the late fourth century, Germanic peoples had penetrated the empire. As the fifth century drew to a close, the Franks brought the existence of Roman Gaul to an end and the Merovingian dynasty under Clovis (481-511) carved out for itself a kingdom centred in an area between the Loire and the Rhine but extending beyond these two rivers into all of south-western France and large areas of Germany. The pragmatic Clovis became a Christian around 500. Since the other Germanic peoples in Gaul were either pagans or followers of the heretic Arius, the Franks therefore gained the support of the Catholic Church. Many of the Franks, and even some of their bishops and clergy, however, were half-hearted about the faith and foreign missionaries had ample scope for evangelisation. Even the most cursory perusal of Gregory's *History of the Franks* can leave the reader in no doubt about the savagery, debauchery and barbarity of Merovingian France.

Following the death of Clovis, the realm was divided among his four sons. As each of these brothers died, the survivors apportioned the newly available lands among themselves. Ultimately this meant that from 558 to 561 all the dynasty's holdings were subject to Clothair I. His death occasioned another quadripartite partitioning of the kingdom: Paris went to Charibert (561-575); Soissons to Chilperic (561-584); Rheims to Sigebert (561-575); and Orléans to Gunthram (561-593). During the next critical decade or so, rivalry between this new generation of brothers led to the appearance of fresh geopolitical units within France. The former kingdom of Rheims, made up of the Rhine, Moselle and Meuse areas, became Austrasia with its capital at

Places with Irish associations in seventh-century Europe

Metz. Neustria emerged from the fusion of part of the kingdom of Soissons and a portion of the kingdom of Paris. It was initially ruled from Soissons but later, when that city was ceded to Austrasia, from Paris. Orléans, minus its western districts, was added to Burgundy by which name the kingdom thenceforward was known. Gunthram, its 'good king', transferred his capital to Chalon-sur-Saône. The Burgundians, a kindred Germanic people, were assimilated by the Franks.

There was bitter rivalry between the consorts of two of these kings. The feud between Brunhilda, Sigebert's queen, and Fredegund, Chilperic's wife, brought violent deaths to their husbands. The peaceful acquisition of Burgundy by Austrasia in 593 extended Brunhilda's control, through her son, Childebert II (575-595), and then her grandsons, to both kingdoms. By the end of the sixth century France was divided into two rival power-blocks: north-western Gaul (Neustria), controlled by Clothair II (584-629), the son of Chilperic and Fredegund; and northern and eastern Gaul, in the hands of Brunhilda and her progeny, with her elder grandson Theudebert (595-612) ruling as king of Austrasia while his brother Theuderic II (595-613) reigned over Burgundy.

After a disastrous war between Brunhilda's bellicose and fratricidal grandsons and on her own ignominious death in 613, Clothair II, King of Neustria, obtained Burgundy and Austrasia. France was once more united with Paris as its capital. Although his son Dagobert (629-639) was able to maintain this unity, subsequent Merovingians proved ineffectual. One of them, Clovis III, typical of his clan, was nick-named le Fainéant or 'Do-nothing'! In this vacuum, rivalry began again between the territories. In both Neustria and Austrasia power was in the hands of the major dukes, the so-called Mayors of the Palace: Erchinoald and later Ebroin in Neustria and Pepin II in Austrasia. In 687 Pepin II managed to take control of Neustria and Burgundy. Theoretically representatives of the Merovingians continued to reign over the reunited France during most of the first half of the eighth century, but power had actually passed into the hands of the Pepinids. In 751, Pepin III, 'the Short', deposed the last of the enfeebled Merovingians and the Carolingians took the Frankish throne.

In the last decade of the sixth century, then, France was made up of three kingdoms – Austrasia, Neustria and Burgundy. Although these regions were nominally Christian in 591, religious practice there lacked much of the fervour and discipline which Columban had known in his homeland. The saint set to work, therefore, with a sense of urgency. He made his first foundation at Annegray in the Vosges Mountains on the border between Austrasia and Burgundy.

The site he chose had once been a Roman fort and was adapted by Columban to suit his purposes, with the old Temple of Diana being transformed into a chapel for his community. Very rapidly the fame of Columban spread. Men from every social stratum joined him. His following increased so much that he was forced to establish a second monastery at Luxeuil, eight miles west of Annegray, and this was soon to become his most important foundation. But even this did not meet the demand which he generated and as more disciples flocked to his side he was required to set up another monastery at Fontaines, only three miles to the north of Luxeuil. The *Life of Saint Valericus* states that the number of disciples in Columban's three French houses was two hundred and twenty. It was at this stage that Columban drew up for his communities his *Monks' Rule*, by which their actions and attitudes were to be governed, and his *Community Rule*, detailing punishments for breaches of it. He also drew up a penitential for both lay and religious penitents.

Columban, quite wittingly no doubt, incurred the wrath of the French hierarchy. Monks in late sixth-century France were forbidden to set up monasteries without the consent of the local ordinary; an abbot was not permitted to have jurisdiction over more than one house; and a religious superior was not allowed to rule in an independent manner (there was no 'monastic exemption' in late sixth-century France) but only in conjunction with his bishop. Columban chose to ignore all these restrictions. On top of this, in determining the date of Easter, the Irishman followed a paschal cycle at variance with that being used in his host country. Columban in this fashion aroused the antipathy of the French bishops and came into confrontation with them.

In 600, with typical decisiveness, determining that attack was the best form of defence, the missionary took the initiative and wrote to Pope Gregory defending his position. There is no evidence of the Pope having responded to Columban's missive, though he does seem to have placed the Irishman under the protection of the abbot of Lérins. In 603 the bishop of Lyons, the doyen of the French bishops, demanded Columban's presence at a council in Chalon. This he refused to attend, sending instead a defiant and witheringly sarcastic letter, outlining his position.

Events then began to turn more against the saint when he brought upon himself the hostility of the Burgundian king. The death of Childebert II in 595 had put his two sons, Theuderic II and Theudebert, on the thrones of Burgundy and Austrasia respectively. These infants were under the protective eye of their grandmother, Brunhilda.

Relations between Theuderic and Columban appear to have been friendly until the young king's marriage broke down in 609 and the saint refused to bestow his blessing upon the monarch's illegitimate sons. Columban found himself in an untenable position. He was arrested, removed from Luxeuil and escorted to Besançon. After a short stay there he slipped back to Luxeuil where, having been punished, he hoped to be left in peace. He had not yet, however, paid the full price for his tenacity. When the king heard of the return of the meddlesome priest he took extreme action: this time Columban and his Irish monks were to be sent back to Ireland. An eventful, six-hundred-mile trek across France brought the Irishmen and their guards to Nantes where Columban and his companions were put on board a ship bound for Ireland. The ship set sail. The soldiers departed. And then providence intervened! The boat was driven aground and the captives found themselves free once more.

Resolving to avoid further confrontation with Theuderic, Columban set off northwards to the court of King Clothair of Neustria. He advised the king not to become involved in the civil war which had broken out between Theuderic and Theudebert. From there Columban headed to Metz, the capital of Austrasia, and was warmly received by King Theudebert and some of his community from Luxeuil, including Eustasius. The saint and his Irish monks next moved east to make a new settlement at Bregenz on the eastern side of Lake Constance, in the modern Austrian-Swiss border region. Here they remained for about a year until, in 612, their protector Theudebert, who had ignored the prescient warnings of Columban, was defeated in battle by his brother Theuderic. Vulnerable once more, the ageing Columban was forced to leave Bregenz and to lead his followers into Italy. Gall, his trusted friend and once-faithful disciple, however, was reluctant to accompany him. Jonas does not say why but Walahfrid Strabo, who wrote a *Life of Gall* in the ninth century, states that his hero had fallen 'suddenly ill of a fever'. Columban felt that his disciple was malingering and ordered Gall never to celebrate Mass again as long as Columban himself should live. On this sour note they parted and in the autumn of 612 Columban set out to take his loyal band on the arduous journey across the Alps to Milan.

Here, at the court of the duke of Lombardy, Columban became involved once again in contention. Duke Agilulf was an Arian, like most of his subjects, but his wife and son were Catholics. The duke invited the saint to remain in his territory which Columban did but, true to his character, he did not condone Arianism. It was probably at this point in his career that Columban delivered the thirteen sermons which have survived. These lengthy homilies are all heavily trinitarian in doctrine and so, by implication, sharply anti-Arian.

From Milan Columban wrote to Boniface IV, a weak occupant of the papal throne with possible schismatic tendencies. In Columban's opinion this Pope was not taking a strong enough lead in the *Three Chapters* controversy, an episode in the long conflict between the Monophysites and the Nestorians concerning the divinity/ humanity of Christ. But Columban was tiring and all of this must have been wearisome for a septuagenarian, a man who had left Ireland many years before, who had travelled hundreds of miles on the continent and who would have preferred to express his love of Christ through solitude, contemplation and prayer. And so, when he was offered a resting place by Agilulf, seventy miles south of Milan on the banks of the Bobbio, he gladly accepted. Bobbio was to be Columban's final monastic settlement and although he was invited to return to Gaul by King Clothair, who had succeeded in reuniting the three strife-torn Frankish kingdoms, he refused. At Bobbio he remained until, after sending his forgiveness to his friend Gall, he died on Sunday, 23rd November, 615.

What can we say about the significance of Columban? His foundation at Luxeuil had a colossal impact on the religious history of France and numerous seventh-century religious personages were associated with it or were influenced personally by its founder. Some of these were members of the group of twelve who accompanied Columban from Ireland: for instance, Gall, the apostle of Switzerland; Domoal, the abbot's secretary; and Deicolus, who was too ill in 610, when Columban fell foul of King Theuderic, to go with his master into exile and whose hermitage in Burgundy ultimately grew into the great abbey of Lure, the second abbot of which was to be Columban the Younger. Some were people upon whom Columban had an enormous effect, in what were perhaps to him rather insignificant encounters with mere children: for example, Chagnoald, Faro and their sister Burgundofara, bishop of Laon, bishop of Meaux and foundress of the convent of Faremoutiers, respectively; and Ouen, the future chancellor of two Merovingian kings, then founder along with his brothers of the monastery of Rebais, and finally bishop of Rouen. Some were prominent citizens, courtiers and royal officials, the directions of whose lives were radically changed by contact with Columban or his disciples: Didier, ex-treasurer of Clothair II, and a mid-seventh-century bishop of Cahors; and Philibert, founder of the noble monasteries of Jumièges, Noirmoutier, Quincay (near Poitiers) and Montivilliers and of the convent of Pavilly, among whose disciples was an Irish monk named Sidonius. Others were alumni of Luxeuil who set up their own foundations elsewhere bringing the traditions of the mother house and of its founder with them: Mommelin, a monk of Luxeuil, then abbot of Sithiu, and eventually successor of Eloi as bishop of Noyon; Walaric, formerly the gardener at Luxeuil, founder of the monastery of Leucone on the Somme and a most effective missionary in the Pas-de-Calais; and Agile, a disciple of Eustasius of Luxeuil and first abbot of Ouen's Columbanian monastery of Rebais. Through his disciples and those they in turn inspired, then, Columban exercised a huge influence. These men and women were to ensure that monasticism flourished in Carolingian France.

Columban was above all a scholar and a writer. As such he has had a lasting significance. And it is from those of his own writings which have survived that we can know him as a person. Much of the first half of Columban's life was spent in the monasteries of Cleenish and Bangor where he was primarily engaged in the work of education. His early writings were produced in this context and developed automatically from his role as a teacher. His earliest work, the lost *Commentary on the Psalter*, was a text-book, intended for private circulation among his pupils only. In the second half of his life he wrote extensively for much wider audiences in several different genres.

This great output was, however, only a part of his daily routine. His first duty remained prayer and meditation on the scriptures which is central to the monk's life. These important habitual responsibilities did, of course, influence his thought and the content of what he wrote. For each of the genres in which he wrote Columban used a style suited to it; he wrote with intelligence, flexibility and adaptability. His sermons are rhetorical in tone, if perhaps too wordy and attention-seeking. His letters are much more chatty and are subtly tailored to the character and status of their recipients. 'From the literary point of view,' as Walker remarks, the poem *Columbanus to his Brother Fidolius* 'forms the crown of Columban's achievement.' It is charming, cheerful, rhythmic and composed in clear, coherent Latin. His other poems reveal no new insights and are pedestrian but do have a certain muscular clarity. Finally, his legislative works – his *Rules* and *Penitential* – are typical of such documents, being concise, dry and doctrinaire {Note 1}.

Columban was not writing without models and he borrowed freely from his predecessors and contemporaries. He could quote Ovid, Juvenal, Martial, Sallust and other classical authors of antiquity, but especially Virgil and Horace. He was well-read in some of the late Latin writers like Prudentius and Fortunatus. This acquaintance with acknowledged works of merit provided him with a literary yardstick by which he could assess his own output. He was familiar with classical mythology and would seem even to have known the meanings of a limited number of words in Greek and Hebrew. As a churchman he had a wide knowledge of the Fathers and other ecclesiastical writers. He was acquainted with the writings of Cassian and Jerome, above all, but had obviously also read Basil – the source of much of his legislative writing – Augustine, Pope Gregory the Great, Finnian (for his *Penitential*) and Eusebius. As a monk he was steeped in the scriptures. Naturally, since he recited it daily, he was most conversant with the psalter but he also knew intimately the New Testament (especially Matthew, Luke, John, Romans, 1 Peter and 1 Corinthians) and the Book of Isaiah from the Old Testament. Western culture owes him an enormous debt because he helped preserve the writings of classical antiquity and simultaneously familiarised his readers with the scriptures and the works of some of the great Christian thinkers.

Just as we can only capture the real Saint Patrick by examining his authentic writings, so can we best discover Columban through his literary works. Our picture of the man can also, of course, be enhanced by the revelations in Jonas. From these sources, Columban emerges as a methodical and painstaking individual, unoriginal and humourless but strikingly competent. A man of absolute determination, he could be described by the unsympathetic as ruthless and by the sympathetic as unsentimental. Having identified his goal, he pursued it relentlessly. He had a quixotic side to his nature and seems to have enjoyed championing minority causes. He was intimidated by no one and had the confidence to confront and, if necessary, correct both high and low. He also had the unusual gift of empathy. We find him participating in games with infants and putting ex-convicts and mercenaries at their ease. He was a born leader, direct and decisive, commanding respect and winning loyalty. He always spoke his mind. Above all, his was an inviolable integrity.

Some of the Church's saints, although men and women of heroic holiness, seem strange and even a little frightening to the twentieth-century observer. Their lifestyles and attitudes belong to a particular age and culture. Their practices may even seem remote and bizarre, and their horizons limited. When we analyse the character of Columban, however, we discover someone – albeit gigantic in stature – strikingly contemporary: a man of action, perception, shrewdness, bluntness, courage and tenacity. It is little wonder that he is still acknowledged as one of a handful of Irishmen who have contributed significantly to the history of western Europe. For the Christian, the recognition won and retained by this 'blind westerner', as he calls himself in his letter to Pope Gregory the Great, should by no means be surprising for he had committed himself, 'warts and all', to

Christ.

This sketch of the political background and of the career and character of Columban leads to a treatment of the activities of other heroic Christians of the Irish tradition in the Merovingian Empire. But first a caution! Columban was so highly regarded that as time passed almost every significant religious figure in much of western Europe was truthfully or fictitiously linked to the saint and to Ireland by early hagiographers. To avoid exaggerating the achievements of Irish monks and their disciples in this part of the world it is necessary to concentrate on personalities about whose Irishness there is reasonable confidence.

Columban was the foremost of the Irish *peregrini* on the continent but he was neither the first nor the only Irish missionary to work in western Europe, especially in France. Tradition has it that early in the sixth century a number of Irish religious *emigrés* were working purposefully in Gaul. Gibrian and his nine sibling-companions laboured in the forests along the Marne on the invitation of Remigius, bishop of Rheims. Berthold, founder of a monastery which was to form the nucleus of the medieval city of Chaumont, and the hermit Amandus, who made an impact in the area around Beaumont, also had the patronage and support of Remigius who died in 533.

Irish zeal and practices were imported into Picardy and Flanders, in what is now the extreme north of France and Belgium but which was then an integral part of the Frankish state, along a number of channels but primarily by the 'Burgh Castle Group': Fursa, Foillan, Ultán and their associates. Right through the sixth century Irishmen worked as evangelists in this region but it was with the arrival of Fursa and the beginning of Irish associations with Péronne that Irish influence became paramount in Picardy and Flanders. Little is known about Fursa's activity in France except that he founded the abbey of Lagny on the river Marne, north of Paris. He was welcomed and assisted by Erchinoald, Mayor of the Palace of Neustria. He died at Mazerolles (Somme) in 649.

A number of Irishmen, other than his brothers Foillan and Ultán, are linked with Fursa: notably, Eloquius, his successor as abbot of Lagny; Goban, who was martyred in the middle of the seventh century; and Madelgisel, a hermit of Ponthieu. It was only in 654, when Fursa's incorrupt body was transferred to a specially built shrine at Péronne, that an Irish colony grew up there and gradually became influential. Foillan, forced to flee England, founded a monastery at his brother's tomb. Later Foillan went into what is now Belgium to establish a monastery at Fosses, on land given to him by Itta and

Early Stone Cross at Reask, Co Kerry
Photo: courtesy Office of Public Works, Dublin

her daughter Gertrude, joint-foundresses of the double monastery of Nivelles, an institution obviously run on Irish lines. Foillan was murdered at Serette by robbers around 655. Three centuries later Fosses was still being described as 'the Irish monastery'. His brother Ultán had succeeded him at Péronne. Ultán's successor was the Irishman Abbot Cellan, correspondent with the Anglo-Saxon scholar-bishop Aldhelm, and Irish associations may have continued with *Peronna Scottorum* ('Péronne of the Irish') until its destruction by the Vikings around 880. About 660 the English born Saint Bathild, who was the titular Merovingian queen and a former slave of Erchinoald, established a monastery at Corbie and a convent at Chelles, both of which would appear to have used an Irish monastic rule.

In the middle and later decades of the seventh century, when the impact of Columban was still making itself felt and when the 'Burgh Castle Group' was successfully active in Picardy and Flanders, a number of comparatively unknown Irishmen were working independently in France. Caidoc and Fricor, two Irish priests, converted Riquier, a Frankish nobleman. He, in turn, established the abbey of Centula, in the town now named after him. Killian of Aubigny is recognised as the patron of the Artois region. The name of his cousin Fiacre, whose hermit's cell became the monastery of Breuil near Meaux, has gone into the French language as the word for a hansom-cab since the terminus for these particular vehicles in seventeenth-century Paris was a hotel named after this Irishman. Fiacre's patronage – along with that of Saint Denis (the patron saint of Paris!) – is sought by those who suffer from syphilis, which the English used to call the 'French Disease' and the French used to refer to as the 'English Disease', and also by gardeners and taxi-drivers. During the late seventh century, in what were the final decades of the Merovingian dynasty, the Irish continued to exert an influence upon the French. One of the last of the Merovingian kings, Dagobert II, spent some twenty years as a reluctant exile in Ireland during a period of unusually severe civil strife in France. His return to Austrasia in 676 saw some of the 'Irish' there in opposite camps. Philibert of Jumièges and Noirmoutier, for example, favoured Dagobert while Ouen, the bishop of Rouen, and Ultán, abbot of Péronne, allied themselves with Ebroin and the opposition. During the civil war Ebroin was for a period an unwilling 'guest' at Luxeuil!

Some Irish missionaries went even further afield, bringing the faith to the pagan and half-pagan Germanic peoples of what are now central and south-west Germany, Switzerland and north-west Austria, then on the eastern frontiers of the Frankish empire.

Switzerland, fully incorporated fully into the Roman empire in 15BC, had been partially converted in the third century and was substantially Christian by the middle of the fourth. It was in this period that the earliest dioceses were established. During the migrations of the Germanic tribes, the Burgundians (c 443) occupied the western and south-western parts of Switzerland. They adopted the tongue and customs of the native Romanic (or French-speaking) population and, although they were Arians initially, there was no serious interruption to the life of the Church. At the beginning of the sixth century the Burgundian king and people adopted the Catholic faith. From 534 the entire territory of the Burgundians belonged to the kingdom of the Franks and shared its religious development. In the fifth century the Alamanni had subjugated the north and north-east of the country. They were heathens and destroyed both the Roman civilisation and the organisation of the Church in the area. At the beginning of the sixth century all Switzerland, north of the Alps, came under the control of the Franks. The diocese of Constance was set up for the Alamanni and a certain amount of spasmodic evangelisation took place.

The territory was, however, open to Irish missionary activity. Columban worked in the area around Bregenz (now just across the border in Austria), on the shores of Lake Constance. After his departure for Italy, his labours were continued in that territory by his former pupil at Bangor, and later insubordinate companion, the saint-linguist Gall. Gall had a hermitage at Arbon and the friendship of a lone local priest named Willimar. He turned down the abbacy of Luxeuil and the bishopric of Constance. He evangelised the semi-pagan inhabitants of much of what is now the diocese of St Gallen in the north-east of the country close to Lichtenstein. It would seem that he had the assistance of a companion called Magnus. Gall died about 640 but his cult continues to this day in the city, diocese and canton which enshrine his name. The bear, which legend has it came out of the woods to help him build his hermitage, is still to be seen in the arms of the city of St Gallen. A great Benedictine monastery, also dedicated to him, was set up about a hundred years after the saint's death. It survived until the early nineteenth century and its church is now a cathedral. Further Trojan work in the conversion of eastern Switzerland was done by Sigisbert, one of Columban's disciples at Luxeuil and his companion at Bregenz, and the monks of the famous abbey of Dissentis which Sigisbert founded around 612 in the Grisons Mountains along the Hither Rhine.

A number of other Irish monks laboured in Bavaria, Franconia and Thuringia, Germanic satellite provinces of the Merovingians. The most famous were: Fridolin, founder of a monastery at Säckingen on the Rhine near Basle; Wendelin, apostle of the territory between the Rhine and the Moselle, out of whose hermitage near Trier the abbey of Tholey developed; and Killian, an Irish bishop who is said to have gone to the continent with eleven companions and to have been done to death at Würzburg in southern Thuringia in 689 along with his co-workers, Colman and Totnan, for daring to admonish the adulterous King Gozbert.

The efforts of Irish *peregrini* during the sixth and seventh centuries in Italy, south of the Merovingian empire, must also be acknowledged. Italy had been invaded from the Balkans in 488 by the barbarian army of the Ostrogoths, accompanied by some three hundred thousand prospective settlers. The Ostrogoths were defeated and dispersed in 553 by the Byzantines and the whole of Italy returned to direct dependence on the Roman emperor now resident at Constantinople. Italy was no longer a centre of power but a provincial outpost with its capital at Ravenna and not Rome. In 568 a new Teutonic people, the Lombards, invaded the peninsula. The Lombards had a truncated, independent kingdom or duchy in northern and central Italy for two centuries until they, too, were overthrown by Charlemagne in 774. Whereas other barbarian invaders had respected the Roman political and administrative structure, the Lombards did away with it in favour of their own institutions. Simultaneously, the Byzantines ruled much of Italy. They controlled Venetia, the Exarchate of Ravenna, Naples, Calabria, Bruttium, and the islands of Sicily, Sardinia and Corsica.

Columban's foundation at Bobbio stood near the lines of communication between the Lombard and Byzantine territories. Bobbio was never predominantly Irish in character but had a Celtic flavour throughout the seventh century {Note 2}. Early in the eighth century an Irish bishop called Cummian spent the final years of his life at Bobbio and is buried there.

More than fifty years ago, Fra Anselmo Tommasini published a book called *Irish Saints in Italy* (London, 1937). Tommasini sketches the careers of supposed Irish missionaries in that part of Europe. One of the men he mentions is Ursus of Aosta, who seems to have come to Italy from Ireland about a century before Columban made the same journey. Like Columban, he was embroiled in the Arian controversy, for the Ostrogoths were either supporters of this particular heresy or were totally pagan. He died in 529. Tommasini claims that another sixth-century evangelist who worked in Italy was Irish – Fridian, bishop of Lucca, one of the heroes of Pope Gregory the Great and another active opponent of Arianism. The Lombards were now the chief supporters of this heresy in the Italian peninsula. A celebrated miracle-worker and ascetic who formed his cathedral chapter into a religious order, Fridian died in 588 {Note 3}. The church at Lucca still celebrates the memory of the obscure Saint Pellegrinus ('Saint Stranger'), supposedly an influential seventh-century Irish hermit. Pellegrinus is venerated, too, in the diocese of Modena. We must also mention the career of Saint Cathald of Taranto. He would seem to have been an Irish bishop (probably in a monastery and possibly that of Lismore, Co Waterford) who went on pilgrimage to the Holy Land about the year 666. On his return journey, he was invited – just as his contemporary, the wily placeman, Wilfrid, was offered the bishopric of Strasbourg in the next decade – to fill the vacant see of Taranto in the Byzantine territory of Calabria in the 'Heel of Italy', a church which he served with distinction as a most reforming prelate until his death some fifteen years later.

It is interesting to observe that native Irish monk-missionaries were not the only medium of transporting Irish influence to western Europe in our period. Many English *peregrini*, trained and inspired in Ireland, went to the continent where they exercised a pronouncedly 'Irish' influence. Bede gives us much information about them. We name but one: Willibrord, apostle of the Frisians. Born in 658 and educated and formed in Ireland, he went on *peregrinatio*, founded the noble monastery of Echternach, became bishop of Utrecht in 695 and died in 739. Willibrord was in turn the teacher of Boniface, who was the chief apostle of Germany and an Englishman who had a profound influence on the history of Europe,

Information about many of these saints is extremely scant. There are no regular biographies of the vast majority of them. Scholars have to attempt to piece together incidental snippets of information from diverse sources – lives of contemporary European figures with whom they came in contact, chronicles, documents of a diplomatic character, monastic annals, letters, poems and so forth. Nevertheless, it is obvious that the Irish *peregrini* and their disciples made an enormous impact on western Europe in the sixth and seventh centuries. What is most apparent is that Columban stood head and shoulders above all his contemporary Irishmen, each of them significant in his own right, in this vast mission territory. He worked with titanic energy for a mere twenty-four years in France, Switzerland, Austria and Italy and inspired followers to toil in places which he himself did not manage to reach. Many of these personages are still remembered in the local cults of the countries of their adoption. Some of them have had a lasting influence on the historical development of western Europe. Columban, and to a lesser extent many of the other Irish missionaries, spearheaded the growth of monasticism in this vast area and brought about a reformation of the Church there. They helped establish on the continent certain Irish ecclesiastical institutions, approaches and values – auricular confession, private penance and penitential literature; the independence of abbots, monks and monasteries from diocesan control; a respect for classical culture and the determination to preserve vulnerable ancient manuscripts; a love of learning and penmanship. Western Europe truly owes a debt to these Irish pioneers of Christianity in the Dark Ages.

Notes:

1. The *Rules* are referred to in Chapter Five. Chapter Ten deals with the Irish penitentials.

2. As we shall see in Chapter Twelve, manuscripts of this period, which survive from the scriptorium of the monastery, have certain prominent Irish features.

3. Many modern scholars are suspicious about the Irish origins of this saint and question a sixth-century *floruit*.

The Irish Penitentials

*'The time is ripe and I repent
every trespass, O my Lord.
Pardon me my every crime,
Christ, as Thou art merciful.'*

[Poem by Óengus Céile Dé;
late tenth century]

In the Catholic Church to-day penance is defined as a sacrament, instituted by Christ, for the purpose of reconciling the sinner to God as often as that sinner falls into sin after baptism. Reflecting the time-honoured practices of the Church, the rite of penance consists of three acts of the penitent – contrition, confession and satisfaction – and the words of absolution said by the priest,'I absolve you from your sins in the name of the Father and of the Son and of the Holy Spirit.' Even in the twentieth century, the penitent still has to have that 'heartfelt sorrow and aversion for the sin committed along with the intention of sinning no more' demanded by the Council of Trent; has to confess to a priest; has to accept a 'penance', an act of mortification or devotion imposed by the confessor, and ultimately perform it; and the priest, the minister of God, has formally to absolve the sinner.

Basic to Catholic teaching on the sacrament of penance is the belief that the ministry of divine pardon was first exercised by Christ [see Mt 9:1-8, for example] and that it was entrusted by Christ to his apostles and their successors in the episcopacy [see Mt 16:19 and 18:18]. In Jn 20:22-23 we see the power promised in Matthew being conferred. Thus the apostolic ministry of forgiveness is regarded as the continuation of Christ's own ministry. When the Church, through its representative, forgives, God forgives (provided, of course, that the penitent has the proper dispositions). This has been the approach of the Church since its beginnings: as the Sacred Congregation for Divine Worship stated in 1973, 'The Church has faithfully celebrated the sacrament throughout the centuries – in varying ways, but retaining its essential elements.'

The penitential practice of the primitive Church followed the example of Saint Paul [see 1 Cor 5:5 and 2 Cor 2:10] in first excommunicating the sinner (the power of binding) and then later in reconciling him (the power of loosing) to the community. The first step in the discipline was confession by the contrite penitent, either to the bishop or, in more densely populated churches like Rome or Antioch, to the priest-penitentiary. The confession of sins was usually private. After confession the sinner made satisfaction for sins by doing public penance. For the purpose, the sinner enrolled in the order of penitents, an order corresponding to that of the catechumens. Like catechumens, penitents had to leave the Sunday liturgy before the Prayer of the Faithful and so could not participate in it or in the Eucharistic Sacrifice that followed. In private, penitents were expected to fast, intensify their prayers and give more generously to the poor. The penitents wore sackcloth, symbolising their separation from Christ's flock [see Mt 25:32-33], and covered themselves in ashes to commemorate Adam's expulsion from paradise and to demonstrate their own exclusion from the Church. In the Roman Church contrite sinners confessed their sins on Ash Wednesday and were excommunicated. The public penance was carried out during Lent. Absolution was extended on Holy Thursday at the Offertory of the Mass after which the penitents were re-admitted to the Eucharist, the sacrament of Christian unity and especially, on this occasion, the joyful banquet of God's Church held to celebrate the return of the prodigal son.

In the early Church, then, the system of penance was most severe. It was performed in public. Furthermore, it could only be undertaken once in a lifetime and certain heavy disabilities went with it: for example, the reconciled sinner was not free to marry or, if already married, to resume sexual relations with a spouse; a male penitent was not permitted to become a cleric in the future, was not allowed to engage in mercantile activity, nor could he enter military service. And so it is not surprising that people did not undergo public penance lightly and that many postponed the ordeal for as long as possible.

Because of the harrowing nature of public penance and the way in which people were postponing its reception, a new form of penance, more accommodating to human frailty, was developed in the sixth century in the churches of Wales and, particularly, Ireland. This new form was private (between penitent and confessor), repeatable and not accompanied by the stiff, life-long penalties associated with public penance. The stimulus for this development may have come from the writings and teachings of Saint Caesarius of Arles, but the sixth-century churches of Ireland and Wales were fertile ground in which it could take root and grow. Monasteries played a very significant part in the lives of these churches. The practices of frequent confession (often of devotion rather than necessity) and public and private spiritual direction for monks were easily adapted to the needs of the laity. Repeated, auricular confession and private penance were soon introduced in Ireland and Wales. From there the new discipline was brought to the Anglo-Saxon kingdoms and to the continent by the *peregrini*. It was not until as late as the eleventh century that absolution was given on the occasion of confession and before the completion of the act of satisfaction, that is, as we have it to-day, prior to the fulfillment of the penance.

The principal features of penitential practice in the Celtic Church were:

(1) The penance was imposed by a private confessor of the penitent's choice.

(2) Most penances were of limited duration and so the sacrament could be resorted to repeatedly.

(3) Penances were graded according to the status of the sinner as well as to the nature of the sin.

(4) Sins of thought as well as of deed were confessed and suitable penances enjoined.

(5) Long penances were often performed in monasteries to which lay penitents temporarily retired {Note 1}.

(6) The system of 'commutation' allowed for the conversion of a lengthy penance into a more moderate one or into one of greater severity but of shorter duration {Note 2}.

(7) Ordinary penances consisted of spells of fasting, often on bread and water, the recitation of psalms or corporal punishment, but alms-giving could be substituted for fasting in cases of infirmity or for other reasons.

It was to spread and facilitate the use of this penitential system that the penitentials, a new genre of religious literature, were introduced. These works reflected and supported the growing practice of private penance. The penitentials assign penances for specific sins. They are manuals or handbooks drawn up for the use of confessors, outlining various sins and apportioning penances for them. Presumably they were for private circulation only: of professional interest to the priest but of no concern whatsoever to the laity. While their chief interest lies in their descriptions of particular sins and their appropriate penances, they are not all merely tariffs for sins. They also reveal, in the guidelines which many of them give confessors, that the sacrament was viewed as 'medicine for souls' to be administered with due regard for the circumstances and dispositions of individual penitents.

Presumably student priests committed particular penitentials to memory. Such an exercise educated the clergyman for the confessional, informing him, as Pierre J Payer speculates, 'of the different kinds of sin, of aggravating and mitigating circumstances, and providing suggestions for appropriate penances.' Once memorised, this material would also assist the confessor in the essential interrogation and possible education of the penitent, to ensure that he had confessed all his serious sins and simultaneously was instructed about the nature of sin {Note 3}. Indispensable to the apprentice priest, the penitentials also acted as salutary reminders to experienced and maybe hardened confessors of the need for sensitivity in the routine of the confessional, where Christ's mercy was to be shown by the minister rather than human legalistic adherence to regulations. The penitentials were, then, primarily pastoral in approach: they dealt with the procedure by which sinners were reconciled to God and the community and they informed, directed and exhorted the priest in his confessional responsibilities.

The penitentials form a large and complex *corpus* of literature. The original body of texts is made up of a number of early Welsh works – technically speaking not proper penitentials but having a penitential character – and the first full penitentials which are of Irish origin. The Welsh texts of relevance are *The Preface of Gildas on Penance, The Synods of North Britain, The Synod of the Grove of Victory* and *The Excerpts from a Book of David.* These four works are the earliest surviving penitential documents of the Celtic Church. The chief early penitentials proper, all of an Irish provenance, are those of Finnian, Columban and Cummean, all in Latin, and the later *Old Irish Penitential,* written in Goidelic {Note 4}.

Finnian's is the earliest extant Irish penitential. It predates the *Penitential of Columbanus* which is heavily dependent on Finnian's work. Columban drew up his penitential on the continent after 591. The *Penitentialis Vinniani (Penitential of Finnian)* was probably composed, for the benefit of his monks, by either Finnian of Clonard, who died in 549, or Finnian of Moville, who died thirty years later in 579. 'Clear in outline but not very careful in detail,' as Bieler remarks, the

Cross Slab at Fahan, Co Donegal
Photo: courtesy Office of Public Works, Dublin

work is made up of fifty-three canons, four prefatory canons on certain sexual misdemeanours of boys and men, and an appendix. In Canon 29 the author states the principle 'by contraries let us make haste to cure contraries'. This penitential approach was originally advocated by Cassian, the influential monk-writer of the early fifth century, and doubtless adopted from medieval medical practice.

The *Penitential of Columbanus*, mainly the work of the saint but with a number of later additions, is a tripartite work dealing with the sins of monks, secular clergy and lay people. Forty-two canons in all, it begins with a short preface [Canon A1] and contains a statement (just before Canon B1) comparing the ministrations of 'spiritual doctors' with those of 'doctors of the body'. Like Finnian, Columban was familiar with Cassian's theory of *contraria contrariis curare* ('curing contraries by contraries'). He may have read Cassian himself or he may have received this insight indirectly through Finnian by whom he was deeply influenced. Bieler is convinced that the nucleus of the work was drawn up in France in the early years of Columban's sojourn in the Vosges Mountains.

The *Penitential of Cummean* is the most all-embracing of the Irish penitentials in Latin. It has two-hundred and three separate subdivisions. A detailed examination of this document gives some appreciation of the form and spirit of this particular type of literature. A tightly-structured work, built around Cassian's ogdoad of deadly sins, Cummean's penitential has chapters on gluttony, fornication, avarice, anger, dejection, sloth, vainglory and pride. These eight chapters are followed by three others: on petty offences, on the sins of boys, and on disrespect for the Blessed Sacrament. Chapter VIII ends with a short list of commutations. The penitential begins with a treatise on the 'twelve remissions of sins', for which the author was indebted to Church Fathers like Origen and Cassian, and ends with an epilogue in which confessors are exhorted to impose penances with due regard to the status and circumstances of each individual sinner. As well as receiving inspiration from patristic sources, Cummean was influenced by the compilers of the four early Welsh texts listed above and to a certain extent by Finnian. Bieler is of the opinion that the author of this penitential was Cuiméne the Tall who, according to the *Annals of Ulster*, 'rested in the seventy-second year of his age' in 662. He was a celebrated hymnist and a bishop of Clonfert.

After his 'Prologue on the Medicine for the Salvation of Souls', Cummean treats of the sin of gluttony, dealing with excessive drinking and over-eating. Those who 'have taken the vow of sanctity' and confess to drunkenness are to be given a penance of 'forty days with bread and water'. Laymen, however, for the same fault receive only 'seven days' [Canon I: 1]. For foolhardy hospitality, leading to the intoxication of a guest, the confessor is required to impose a penance equivalent to that which would be received by the guest himself. But if the intemperance was brought about through malice, the perpetrator is to be 'judged as a homicide' [Canons I: 2 and 3]. A monk who admits to having been tipsy and 'unable to sing psalms, being benumbed and speechless' is to be made to 'perform a special fast' [Canon I: 4]. A monk who acknowledges that he has prematurely eaten a meal or displayed greediness at table is to receive a penance of either the loss of his supper or 'two days on bread and water' [Canon I: 5]. A penitent who confesses to over-eating to the point of 'satiety' is to be made to do penance 'for one day', but if he has gorged himself 'to the point of vomiting, though he is not in a state of infirmity, for seven days' [Canons I: 6 and 7]. If such surfeit has led him to vomit up the Host, then he must do penance 'for forty days' unless he has the extenuating circumstance of infirmity in which case the act of self-mortification shall last 'for seven days'. Reverence towards the Blessed Sacrament even in these circumstances should, however, be recognised and 'if he ejects it into the fire, he shall sing one hundred psalms'. Conversely, reprehensible carelessness towards the undigested Host so that, for example, 'dogs lap up this vomit' should lead to the imposition of a 'penance for one hundred days' [Canons I: 8-11]. Gourmand monks who admit to raiding the monastery larder are to perform penance for 'forty days' for a first offence, for 'three forty-day periods' for a second, 'for a year' for a third, and 'in permanent exile under another abbot' for a fourth [Canon I: 12]. Ten-year-old boys who confess to stealing anything are to 'do penance for seven days' but twenty-year-olds who admit to small thefts are to receive 'twenty or forty days' [Canons I: 13 and 14].

This particular chapter in Cummean shows the discretion and ability to weigh individual circumstances and attitudes demanded of the confessor. It shows, too, the application of the principle of 'curing contraries by their contraries': the greedy man is healed by having to fast, and so on. It is, however, geared almost exclusively to monk-penitents; the laity are referred to only in the final clause of Canon I: 1.

This is not the case in the chapter which deals with fornication where some of the sexual sins of lay people are discussed along with those of bishops, priest-monks, monks, and secular clergymen. The layman who repents 'fornication and the shedding of blood', for example, 'shall do penance for three years; in the first, and in three forty-day periods of the others, with bread and water, and in all [three years] without wine, without meat, without arms, without his wife' [Canon II: 22]. The adulterous layman or he who defiles his neighbour's 'virgin [daughter] shall do penance for one year with bread and water, without his own wife' [Canon II: 23]. A layman who seduces a nun 'shall do penance one year and one-half without delicacies and without his wife' but if he confesses to having left her with child ('a son') he 'shall do penance for three years without arms; in the first, with bread and water, in the others without wine and meat' [Canons II: 24 and 25]. A layman who admits in confession to having had sexual intercourse with 'his woman slave' has to 'sell her and do penance for one year' but if he has had 'a son by her, he shall set her free' [Canons II: 26 and 27]. Sterile couples (though the penitential author, obviously the product of a male chauvinist society, merely refers to the barrenness of the wife) are expected to 'live in continence' [Canon II: 28]. It is presumed that all couples will practise continence during the three Lenten seasons each year, on Saturday and on Sunday, night and day, and in the two appointed weekdays, and after conception, and during the menstrual period to its very end' [Canon II: 30]. Post-parturitive abstinence is also required: after a male child for thirty-three days; after a female baby for sixty-six days [Canon II: 31]. A woman who admits to having left her husband for a period of time is expected to 'do penance for one year with bread and water', and similarly her husband, if he has in the meantime 'taken another wife'. He is to receive his wife back 'without payment' [Canon II: 29].

Some of these approaches seem strange to the twentieth-century reader. They are very much the product of their time, dominated as it was by Saint Augustine's teaching that celibacy was preferable to conjugal life and that sex was proper to marriage (which, of course, all practising Christians must hold) and solely ordered to the procreation of children (to which our relatively modern insights into the 'partnership' of marriage no longer confine the marriage act). The influence of the Mosaic Law regarding ritual cleanliness is also very obvious. It must be noted, however, that Irish penances are mild in comparison with the severe, life-long restrictions imposed by the earlier discipline of public penance in the western Church, especially those affecting marriage and the use of marriage.

Both Pierre J Payer and James A Brundage have highlighted the emphasis placed by the authors of the penitentials on sexual sins. Payer, in his sane treatment of *Sex and the Penitentials* (Toronto, 1984), says that 'all of the penitentials contain a great many canons censuring various types of sexual behaviour.' He claims that 'one of the most striking features of the penitentials is the breadth and depth of their treatment of human sexual behaviour.' Payer finds that thirty-seven

Sign ∴ of canons in penitentials deal w. sex

118   THE IRISH PENITENTIALS

protag. on immrama born of sinful union!

per cent of Finnian's work, for instance, contains 'sexually related canons'. Brundage, in his racy but secular and tendentious treatment of the same topic, in *Law, Sex, and Christian Society in Medieval Europe* (Chicago, 1987), comes to the same conclusion: 'Sexual offences constituted the largest single category of behaviour that the penitentials treated'.

Criticism of penitentials.

This prominence made scholars of earlier generations shy away from these texts. The reactions of some of them have been extreme. Charles Plummer, for example, found the penitential literature 'a deplorable feature of the medieval Church. Evil deeds, the imagination of which may perhaps have dimly floated through our minds in our darkest moments, are here tabulated and reduced to system. It is hard to see how anyone could busy himself with such literature and not be the worse for it.' And Nora Chadwick viewed them as spurious inventions bearing no relationship to actual sexual mores: 'webs spun in the casuistry of the monkish brain ... an abstract compendium of supposititious crimes and unnatural sins, thought up in the cloister by the tortuous intellect of the clerical scribe.' Although Kathleen Hughes [1966] did not consider the penitentials 'likely to have a morally harmful influence on anyone' and found them potentially 'extremely boring', she believed them to have been composed in good faith but comprehensive to the point of unreality as they 'attempt to list everything.' Even Ludwig Bieler [1963] (whose edition of the Irish penitentials, in Payer's estimation, 'is really the only entirely trustworthy edition to date') dismissed their treatment of certain types of human sexual behaviour as bearing 'little relation, if any, to reality.' He was of the opinion that 'a great deal of all this would seem to owe its existence to a desire for material completeness and a delight in subtle distinctions and classifications, which is a notorious weakness of the legal mind.'

Modern authorities are not so myopic and are doubtless more realistic. They view the penitentials as having been produced in and for a real-life context. The confessional is not a vicarage tea-party. The confessor in his lifetime will listen to many unsavoury stories and, while the priest does not expect to meet a murderer or a rapist every time he draws back the shutter in his confession-box, he must, however, be prepared for every eventuality. There *are* murderers, rapists and drunkards; some unfortunates commit or are subjected to incest. The confessor has to be ready to receive whomsoever the grace of God directs to his box. The same has been true down through the ages. We are all tainted with Original Sin. And so the priest in the early Middle Ages, then as now, had to be trained to deal with all the possible cases that he would have to confront in his active ministry.

Mention of homicide, or perjury, or blasphemy, or bestiality, or whatever in the penitentials tells us nothing about the frequency or popularity of these particular aberrations at the time the books were drawn up. The penitentials were compiled for the use of confessors, not as reference-books for the prurient or even for modern historians interested in anthropology or sociology. They cannot, therefore, be used to support theories about the warping nature of single-sex institutions like monasteries or the prevalence of bestiality in a sparsely-populated, pastoral society like sixth- and seventh-century Ireland. All they show is that human nature does not seem to have changed over the centuries and that confessors in the early Irish Church were equipped to welcome all sinners and reconcile them with the Father.

What do the penitentials reveal to the modern reader? They show that the system of penance practised in the Welsh and Irish Churches was one of auricular confession and private penance. The sinner confessed in private to a priest of his choice, performed his penance in private and finally received absolution. Moreover, the penitentials throw light on the theory and practice of penance. Confession and penance were a 'medicine for souls'. This idea goes back to Christ himself. In Matthew's Gospel we see Our Lord comparing himself to a physician [see Mt 9:12, for example]. The authors of the penitentials viewed penance as a 'medicine' and Christ, in the person of his priest, as the prescribing physician.

The confessor was seen as a 'soul-friend' (or *anamchara*, as he was called in Irish). His job was to apply, in Christ's place, the appropriate remedy to the soul's disease and his penitential was to assist him in his diagnosis and prescription. All the symptoms of each individual case had to be considered by the careful confessor for, though the standard remedies are to be found in the penitential, people and their motives and degrees of temptation differ. Finnian applied one of the maxims of primitive medicine to the cure of souls through the sacrament of penance, 'By contraries ... let us make haste to cure contraries ... Patience must arise for wrathfulness; ...for greed, liberality' [Canon 29]. It was the aim of the penitentials to heal the hurt which results from sin; primarily to heal the hurt done to the sinner, but also the hurt done to the community. Both Finnian and Cummean emphasise this remedial aspect of penance over and above its punitive dimension: that is, the 'curing' of the diseased soul as well as retribution for the offence given to God. Following Gildas, Cummean, for example, permits a priest-monk who has confessed to fornication and received 'penance for seven years' to go to the Eucharist after eighteen months 'lest his soul perish utterly through lacking so long the celestial medicine' [Canon II: 2].

Being 'medicine for souls', the penitentials doubtless had a whole-some influence on daily life. They must have curbed bloody quarrels and feuding. They must have restricted sexual perversion and the use of abortifacients and aphrodisiacs [see Finnian Canons 20, 18 and 19, for instance], and imposed a certain minimum of hygiene [see Cummean, Canons X:18 and XI:12, 14, 15 and 18, for example]. They must also have been a support to the secular law. Sometimes the civil law and the penitentials reflect one another. Nevertheless, these two approach law-enforcement from very different angles. Secular law is interested in protecting rights and in penalising trans-gressors. The penitentials deal with moral evil and aim to cure the sinner.

The penitentials are invaluable for the light they throw on the re-spective roles of monks and secular clergymen in the early Irish Church. For much of this present century scholars so stressed the pre-eminent monastic constitution of the Church in early medieval Ireland that the absolute monastic character of the institution was taken for granted. Indeed, abbots were viewed as having had supreme administrative powers in the Irish Church of our period: bishops were seen as merely necessary appendages, exercising only sacramental functions. This was an exaggerated viewpoint and rela-tively recent scholarship has redressed the balance. Kathleen Hughes, in *The Church in Early Irish Society* (London, 1966), was the first authority to question the conventional wisdom. Since then, both Monsignor Patrick J Corish, particularly in his essay 'The Pastoral Mission in the Early Irish Church' [1971], and the late Father John Ryan, in his introduction [1972] to the second edition of his standard work on the origins and development of Irish monasticism, have built on the foundations laid by their enterprising English colleague.

Because of their penetrating scholarship, it is no longer possible to ignore the pastoral work of local, non-monastic clergy in the Irish Church for the first three hundred years of its existence. Admittedly, for its first six centuries the Church in Ireland was markedly monastic in character and from the Viking onslaught until the twelfth-century reform it would seem to have been exclusively so. But it was the secular clergy who had the significant pastoral mission in pre-Viking Ireland. The penitentials provide evidence for this. Professor Corish discusses the penitentials of Finnian and Columban and finds that 'a striking feature of both penitentials is that they envis-age the pastoral clergy as non-monastic.' Both works give a crucial role in the reconciliation of a penitent who has completed the act of satisfaction to a bishop or a priest. Above all, Finnian's reference to the failure by negligent clerics to baptise dying children, especially if they are 'of the same parish' [Canons 47 and 48] and his denial to monk-priests of the capacity to administer the sacrament of baptism [Canons 49 and 50] pre-suppose an exclusive pastoral ministry for the secular clergy.

Furthermore, the *Old Irish Penitential*, presumably dating from the late eighth century when the secular clergy was already under threat, legislates for priests and deacons 'who have not taken monastic vows' [Cap.II.8] and regrets the limited numbers of 'persons in orders ... under the hand of a bishop, i.e. a bishop of the tribe' [Cap.II.10]. Collaborative evidence of this situation is to be found in some of the *Lives of the Saints* and in the secular law. In his description of the way in which various groups were segregated during worship in the Great Church, for instance, Cogitosus refers to non-monastic priests (presumably from outlying parishes within Kildare's *termonn*) and laymen occupying a distinct section of the building, separate from the choir which housed the coenobites. Native civil law afforded a bishop the same 'honour price' as a king but gave an abbot, no matter how illustrious, a lesser dignity. Most significantly, the *Ríagail Pátraic (Rule of Patrick)*, an eighth-century document, states that 'every *tuath* should have a chief-bishop, to ordain its clergy, to consecrate its churches, to direct its kings and nobles, and to sanctify and bless their children after baptism.'

The evidence for an active, non-monastic ministry contained in these documents is also confirmed by material to be found in certain canon law texts: the *First Synod of Saint Patrick*, the *Irish Canons*, and the *Second Synod of Saint Patrick*, all of which happily are to be found in Professor Bieler's edition of the penitentials, and the lengthy *Collectio Canonum Hibernensis*, edited by H. Wasserschleben and published in Leipzig in 1885. The *First Synod of Saint Patrick* dates from no later than the mid-sixth century and may, indeed, be contemporaneous with Patrick. The authentic decrees in this work speak of a married clergy [Canon 6], subordinate to the local bishop [Canons 23, 24 and 27], and domiciled rather than vagrant [Canon 3]. From at least the middle years of the 500s, therefore, and presumably from a much earlier date if Patrick's mention of 'a holy presbyter' and 'other clergy' [*Epistola*, 3] is significant, the parochial clergy had a definite function in Irish society. The *Irish Canons*, which Doctor Bieler [1963] believes to be no later than the middle of the seventh century, forbid keening on the death of 'a cleric of the parish' [Canon I.28] and discuss the penalties attaching to physical assaults upon bishops and presbyters [Canons IV.1-9].

The *Second Synod of Saint Patrick*, the product of an unspecified, pro-Roman, seventh-century Irish synod, reveals that at the time of its composition bishops, monks and nuns enjoyed the highest esteem within the local Church, while the clergy, widows and the continent were considered somewhat less worthy but nevertheless superior to all other members of the community [Canon XVIII]. In the interest of parish unity and to defend the rights of local incumbents, this particular piece of legislation also seems to object to monks living outside their monasteries [Canon XX]. The *Second Synod*, then, views the secular clergy as an independent, if inferior, group whose rights in their parishes are not to be infringed by coenobites. The collection of eighth-century Irish canons, as Kathleen Hughes [1972] remarks, 'legislates for a church governed by bishops.' It requires a priest to reside near his church and binds him particularly to be present on Sundays for the people entrusted to his care. The penitentials and allied sources, therefore, make it manifest, as Monsignor Corish demonstrates, that 'until the Norse raids made life impossible for those who were institutionally weak, the non-monastic clergy was regarded as the normal pastoral ministry, and to a great extent functioned as such.'

Finally, we can observe that the penitentials are one of the sources which illustrate Irish connections with Britain and the continent. Cummean used the classification of the eight deadly sins as a framework for his penitential. Both this and the maxim of 'curing contraries by their contraries' show that the basic principles of Irish penitential thinking originated with Cassian and that Irish clerics were familiar with opinions which had been disseminated in southern Gaul in an earlier age. Columban and perhaps other monk-missionaries brought the Celtic penitential system to the continent, where it soon became established. The Anglo-Saxons received it through the *Scotti peregrini*. Even after the Synod of Whitby (664) it was not abandoned. The late seventh- and eighth-century penitential texts that go under the names of Theodore of Canterbury, Bede and Egbert are still in the Irish tradition. Irish penitentials influenced the composition of English penitentials and vice versa. Theodore's penitential, for example, admits to dependence on a *libellus scottorum* ('a little book of the Irish'), which some scholars identify with Cummean, and the *Old-Irish Penitential*, in its turn, quotes from Theodore. Both of these works influenced the creation of the two most comprehensive and best-known Frankish penitentials, the *Escarpsus Cummeani* (*Pseudo-Cummean*) and the *Bigotian Penitential*. Even as late as the eleventh century, and the compilation of the text known as the *Corrector*, this Franco-Insular penitential tradition was flourishing.

The penitentials have been most influential. By recording various types of immorality and calculating commensurate penalties, sins were thereby gauged in terms of their comparative seriousness. This brought about the transmission of a moral code in the early medieval period and into our own era. It is, of course, true that the penitential approach tends to be authoritarian, apodictic and casuistic. This is particularly true of the handling of sexual material in the penitentials and recent western attitudes to sexuality may have been adversely affected by this hair-splitting approach over such a long period of time. This is no reason, however, to denigrate the penitentials themselves. They were composed at a particular time to meet a specific need: the practical need for handbooks of penance. They served their purpose eminently well. Drawn up in an era when neophytes were being wooed away from a still pervasive paganism, they were part of the war-machine of those engaged in combating what Payer describes as the 'urges and forces in human nature which were long in being brought to heel.' They contributed to the diminution in medieval western Europe of the symptoms of heathenism: drunken orgies, promiscuity, licentiousness, murder, wrangling, jealousy, superstition, magic, and so on.

But the penitentials have been even more significant. It is no exaggeration to say that their contribution to the social history of man has been decisive. The penitentials have had a continuing influence on confessional practice. Even a cursory reading of the introduction to the new [1973] *Rite of Penance* and of its 'Form of Examination of Conscience' reveals as much. Furthermore, scholastic theologians and canon lawyers, over the ages, developed the earlier penitential tradition into systems which have had and continue to have an effect on the life of the Church in the twentieth century. Our science of moral theology and Code of Canon Law have been influenced, albeit indirectly, by the Irish penitential system. Even our various Codes of Civil Law may be seen to have been influenced in this way because of the pervasiveness of the Church's jurisprudence and ethical teaching. Finnian, Columban and Cummean have come a long way!

Notes:

1. We know, for instance, that there was a special penitential church at Armagh and that penitents sometimes went to stay with the Columban community on the Scottish island of Inba.

2. Commutation was definitely Irish in origin. The Irish word for it is *arre*, a term which passed into Latin as *arreum*. There is good evidence in the Irish canons that the system was being practised in Ireland as early as the middle of the seventh century.

3. This instruction would, of course, be given by the confessor with a certain circumspection to avoid leading the ill-informed penitent to think about and commit serious sins which he had never before contemplated.

4. Yet again we have to acknowledge a debt to the late Professor Bieler. With the exceptions of the *Old-Irish Penitential* and the *Old-Irish Table of Commutations* which have been reproduced by Dr D A Binchy, Bieler has edited and translated all of the documents in *The Irish Penitentials* (Dublin, 1963; second edition, 1975).

CHAPTER ELEVEN

The Paschal Controversy

'Holy Patrick, then,
celebrating Holy Easter,
kindled the divine fire
with its bright light
and blessed it,
and it shone in the night
and was seen
by almost all the people
who lived in the plain.'

[Muirchú]

The Easter Triduum, when we recall and celebrate the paschal mystery, the great events of Christ's passion, death and resurrection, are the three most important days in the ecclesiastical year {Note 1}. Beginning with the evening Mass of the Lord's Supper on Holy Thursday, continuing through Good Friday with the celebration of the passion of the Lord and Holy Saturday, it reaches its zenith in the Easter vigil and concludes with vespers of Easter Sunday. Pope Leo I called the Easter Triduum *festum festorum* ('the Feast of Feasts').

From at least the second century onwards, the Church celebrated the Easter vigil annually. The Christian Pasch was a nocturnal liturgy, in which the 'passover' from the memory of Christ's passion and death to the joy of his resurrection was made. New converts were baptised during the paschal ceremonies, an activity which underlined the fact that the baptised share in Christ's resurrection and in his divine life. Since Easter was also viewed as the continuation as well as the fulfilment of the Old Testament Pasch, attempts were made to keep to the Jewish lunar calendar in fixing the date of Easter. The Jews celebrated the Passover on the fourteenth day of the March moon, the month of Nisan. Accordingly, this was for the primitive Church the anniversary of the Last Supper. The early Christians

126

remembered the Saviour's death on the fifteenth and his resurrection on the seventeenth. This meant that Easter was celebrated on whichever day of the week the seventeenth happened to fall. Only occasionally would the seventeenth day of the month of Nisan be a Sunday: a fact which, even in the second century, aroused controversy regarding the proper time of observing Easter.

Initially the debate was mainly concerned with the lawfulness of celebrating Easter on a weekday. The Lord's Day was the day on which Christians recalled in their weekly Eucharist the completion of redemption through the resurrection. From about the year 200 on, the general practice was that Easter was celebrated on the Sunday following the fourteenth day of Nisan. Nevertheless, a small group of eastern Christians, the *quartodecimans*, who emphasised the death of Christ, the true Paschal victim, continued to celebrate Easter on the fourteenth day of Nisan. Gradually the *quartodecimans* became more and more isolated until, at the Council of Nicaea in 325, their position was formally rejected and the rule imposed that Easter had to be held on a Sunday.

This did not bring disputes about the dating of Easter to an end. Easter is the centre of the greater part of the Church's year. Even today, a great number of the Sundays and major feast-days depend on the Easter date: the order of Sundays from the first Sunday of Lent to Trinity Sunday; Ash Wednesday; and the feasts of the Ascension, Pentecost and Corpus Christi. The accurate dating of Easter is therefore of crucial importance, a matter of great practical significance to the Church and a sign of disunity if uniformity is not achieved.

But uniformity regarding the determination of the date of Easter was still a long way off. Problems arose for computists when they attempted to reconcile the Jewish calendar, from which the date of the Passover was reached, with the other systems of chronology in use within the Roman empire: the longer Julian calendar, the Egyptian calendar and the Syro-Macedonian calendar. The Jewish calendar was based on the lunar year of three hundred and fifty-four days. The other chronological systems depended on the solar year. Attempts were made to develop a cycle of a fixed number of years so that Easter would occur according to a predetermined pattern in the solar calendars. A sixteen-year cycle introduced in 222 in Rome had to be abandoned because it was imperfect. It was replaced later in the third century by an eighty-four-year cycle. Meanwhile in the east a cycle of nineteen years was devised and this resulted in different dates for Easter in Alexandria and Rome. Circa 454, an effort at reconciliation was made with the introduction of a five-hundred-

and-thirty-two-year cycle (19 x 28), the so-called Victorian Cycle, but this failed to bring together the disputing factions. Unity was not achieved between Alexandria and Rome until a table was constructed by Dionysius Exiguus about 525. Based on the eastern nineteen-year cycle, the Dionysiac Cycle is generally used throughout the Christian world to-day. It has Easter fall on the first Sunday which occurs after the first full-moon following the 21st of March. This means that the earliest possible date of Easter is the 22nd March, the latest the 25th April.

It took a long time for the cycle of Dionysius to find universal acceptance and disputes regarding the dating of Easter continued in the west for more than two centuries, partly as a result of the early introduction into Ireland of a version of the eighty-four-year cycle (the so-called 'Celtic-84') which had quickly become defunct elsewhere in Christendom. This was the tradition taught in the great Irish monasteries of the sixth century. And it was carried by the Irish *peregrini* on their missions to foreign lands. Colum Cille, for example, took it with him to Iona and thence it was introduced to many parts of northern Britain. Columban adhered strictly to the Irish cycle in the heartland of continental Europe. We learn from his writings that he earned the bitter enmity of many of the French bishops when his system conflicted with the one used by them (a usage, incidentally, which was at variance, too, with the Dionysiac Cycle). The dispute on the continent, however, was never as acerbic as it was in Ireland or especially Britain, and after Columban's death in 615 uniformity was gradually and painlessly achieved in mainland western Europe.

Throughout the seventh century pressure mounted upon the Irish to reject their old tradition and accept the authority as well as the practice of Rome. In fact, many began to regard the affair as much more than a dispute about paschal cycles. Bede, who gives a particularly detailed account of the controversy, states that Laurence, Augustine's successor in the see of Canterbury, together with his fellow-bishops Mellitus and Justus, wrote to the Irish hierarchy exhorting them to conform to 'the customs of the universal Church' [ii.4]. Bede also informs us that Pope Honorius (625-638) found it necessary to warn the Irish 'not to consider themselves, few as they were and placed on the extreme boundaries of the world, wiser than the ancient and modern Churches of Christ scattered throughout the earth' [ii.19]. He asked them not to keep a different Easter, contrary to the paschal calculations and synodal decrees of all the bishops of the world.

After this reprimand, a synod was convened at Mag Lena near Birr in 629 or 630. This meeting decided to send a delegation to Rome to try to resolve the issue. The emissaries returned in 632, personally converted to Roman usages. They advocated the adoption of the Roman system in Ireland and many of the churches in the southern part of the island seem at this stage to have conformed. As a result of the meeting at Mag Lena, the pro-Roman Cummian of Durrow wrote (c.632) to Segéne, abbot of Iona, sardonically observing that the entire world was out of step except 'the Britons and the Irish'. But this effort at reconciliation failed too. The northern churches continued to resist change and refused to give up the old Celtic custom even after receiving another sharp rebuke from Rome, this time from the Pope-Elect John IV in 640. Further conflict was unavoidable especially as, in Britain, Celtic monks were evangelising from the north while Roman churchmen were bringing the Good News from the south.

The dispute came to a head in Northumbria in the first half of the sixth decade of the seventh century. There Oswiu was bound by a personal bond of loyalty to the Celtic Church. On the other hand, his wife Eanflaed was a Kentish princess, committed to the Roman tradition. Bede tells us about the confusion which resulted in the royal household: 'Hence it is said that in these days it sometimes happened that Easter was celebrated twice in the same year, so that the king had finished the fast and was keeping Easter Sunday, while the queen and her people were still in Lent and observing Palm Sunday' [iii.25]. This disparity could not continue indefinitely. It must have been unsettling for the royal family and confusing for neophytes. Finan of Lindisfarne, who had succeeded Aidan in 651, was besought by Ronan, an Irish monk, to give up the Celtic practice but to no avail. His successor in 661 at Lindisfarne was Colmán, an equally intransigent Irishman. But forces were massing against the Celtic position. Oswiu's son, Alhfrith, sub-king of Deira, was strongly influenced by Wilfrid who encouraged him to give up his allegiance to the Celtic usage.

Wilfrid, an ex-monk of Lindisfarne who had travelled to Rome, was now a firm advocate of the Roman practice. Won over to the Roman system, Alhfrith displayed his new-found loyalty in 661 by turning out Eata and his monks from the monastery of Ripon because they refused apparently to adopt the Roman custom. The Roman party was further strengthened at this time by the presence in England of the French-born Agilbert, bishop of Dorchester, who supported their cause. Alhfrith persuaded Agilbert to ordain his friend Wilfrid to the priesthood and then bestowed upon him the monastery of Ripon.

The campaign against the Celtic position had turned nasty. Bede, writing at a time when the Roman party had achieved success in Britain, shows the bias of the victor in his account of this incident. He states that Alhfrith rightly preferred the teaching of Wilfrid 'to all the traditions of the Irish' [iii.25] and that the king elevated his protégé at Ripon for he was 'one who was worthy of the place both by his doctrine and his way of life' [iii.25]. Relations between the Irish faction and the Roman party cooled to such an extent that fraternisation between the two groups seems to have ceased.

Wilfrid and Alhfrith, continuing on the offensive, seem to have been instrumental in convening a synod in 664 to settle the matters of dispute between the Roman and Celtic parties in the Church in England. The chief matter at issue was, ostensibly at least, the dating of Easter. Even the location of the Synod at Whitby, then called *Streanaeshalch* (the bay of the lighthouse) which was the chief monastery in the principality of Deira, gave Wilfrid, Alhfrith and their supporters an initial advantage. Whitby, however, was governed by Abbess Hilda who had known Aidan of Lindisfarne and had herself remained loyal to the Celtic tradition.

The *Romani* at the Synod of Whitby were Alhfrith, Wilfrid, Bishop Agilbert, Agatho, James the Deacon and Romanus, who was Queen Eanflaed's chaplain. The *Hibernenses* were represented by Colmán, abbot-bishop of Lindisfarne, and his clerics and by Abbess Hilda. Bishop Cedd 'acted as a most careful interpreter for both parties at the council' [iii.25]. Bede records, in a partisan way, the details of the encounter. King Oswiu, who presided over the meeting, began by calling for unity and the adoption by all of one tradition. Colmán speaking next on behalf of the Irish, stated his case, claiming authority from Saint John. The English-speaker Wilfrid, instead of the more obvious spokesman Agilbert, represented the Roman party and claimed the authority of Saint Peter. He insisted that theirs was a world-wide practice, accepted by everyone save those in the remotest islands. A most eloquent and persuasive debater, Wilfrid demolished Colmán's appeal to the venerability of a usage advocated by Colum Cille. He patronisingly expressed admiration for the achievements of the saint but dismissed his rude simplicity, excused his ignorance on the matter and declared that Colmán, now aware of the practice of the Apostolic See, should have known better. Wilfrid ended by saying that Colum Cille was not to be preferred to Saint Peter to whom Christ had given supreme authority in his Church. Oswiu, rightly convinced that Colum Cille had not been given the same power as Peter, decided in favour of the Roman party with the statement, 'Since he is the doorkeeper I will not contradict him; but I

Carndonagh Cross, Co Donegal
Photo: courtesy Office of Public Works, Dublin

intend to obey his commands in everything to the best of my knowledge and ability, otherwise when I come to the gates of the kingdom of heaven, there may be no one to open them because the one who, on your own showing, holds the keys has turned his back on me' [iii.25].

Easter was not the only issue on the agenda at Whitby. Bede records that at the synod there was 'no small argument' [iii.26] about the shape of the tonsure. Tonsure is the rite of shaving the crown or even the whole head of a man entering the clerical state or the monastic life. The earliest Christian tonsure, possibly dating from the fourth century, entailed the shaving of the whole head. From this the Romans evolved the practice of shaving only the top of the head, possibly in remembrance of the Crown of Thorns. This was different from the form of tonsure used by the members of the Celtic Church.

We are not sure of the exact form of the Celtic tonsure. It may have involved shaving the front of the head in a line in the vertical plane from one ear to the other or it may have meant cropping a cross on the poll leaving four tufts of hair. Edward James believes that as the opposing sides lined up and attitudes hardened regarding the dating of Easter, 'the tonsure came to be seen by individuals on both sides as a way of publicising their allegiance.' Bede does not give details on this particular dispute at the synod but it would appear that when the Roman paschal cycle was accepted in England so, too, was the Roman form of tonsure. The Petrine tonsure was what Doctor James calls 'the outward expression of membership of a single unified church.' We can assume, therefore, that the victorious *Romani* would have insisted on the adoption by all clerics of the English Church of a single style of tonsure as 'a symbol of orthodoxy'.

At least two other issues were raised at the synod: episcopal ordination and baptism {Note 2}. Again, the exact differences in Celtic and Roman practice in the administration of these sacraments are now unknown. It is probable that the Irish permitted the consecration of a bishop by only one other bishop whereas Rome required that the ceremony be performed by three ordaining prelates. Some scholars are of the opinion that the validity of the sacrament of baptism in Ireland was not in question at Whitby but only the fact that the Irish may have omitted the final chrismation. Bede does not relate any of the arguments concerning these matters and the outcome regarding baptism must remain uncertain. We do know, however, that after 664 the Celtic way of episcopal ordination was discontinued.

The decision of the synod regarding the dating of Easter did not meet with immediate or universal acceptance everywhere in the Celtic domain. Although J L Gough Meissner believes that the ascendancy of the Celtic party in Northumbria continued well into the eighth century, we are not convinced that this was indeed the case. Colmán withdrew his monks from northern England, going via Iona to the west of Ireland where he set up monasteries at Inishbofin, for his Irish brethren, and Mayo, for his English followers. His departure left the way clear for the *Romani* in Northumbria to consolidate their position and, as Kathleen Hughes observes, 'a powerful royal authority hurried on the decision' in that kingdom. The Celtic strongholds were reduced to Wales, Iona and the northern part of Ireland. Adomnan, the biographer of Colum Cille and the abbot of Iona, was won over to the Roman cause towards the end of the seventh century but his monks obstinately refused to follow his example. In Ireland he had more success. He persuaded the reluctant clerics of the north to adapt so that the island was probably united behind the Roman usage after the Synod of Birr in 697. Adomnan died in 704 and, after 'a multiplicity of abbots' (A A M Duncan) and much controversy, Iona yielded some twelve years later. Wales, the last bastion of Celtic resistance, conformed in 768.

Whitby must be perceived as much more complex than an argument about the dating of Easter. Religious principles and political considerations were at stake and the different factions within the Northumbrian royal household further complicated the matter {Note 3}. The universality of the Church and the authority of the Pope were at the centre of the dispute. Could the Irish Church insist on retaining a practice honoured by custom but now at variance with the general discipline of the Church? Before the *peregrini* brought the Irish Church into everyday contact with a wider world, the *Hibernenses* had been able to pursue their own independent policy unhindered. They had disturbed or shocked no-one. Contact with Augustine's missionaries in Kent and Columban's dealings with the Franks had automatically brought conflict, scandal and pressure for uniformity. The pressure was, of course, greatest at the points of immediate contact – in France and in Northumbria – where the Irish *peregrini* were in direct confrontation with continental practices. Centralised, strong government in northern England brought a sharp and speedy resolution of the problem there. Geographical remoteness, a climate which permitted the toleration of differences, the absence of a powerful royal authority and the fact that there was no metropolitan to insist on consensus, delayed a settlement in Ireland and took much of the ferocity and acrimony out of the debate there.

The effect of the synod on the Celtic Church was monumental.

Whitby essentially marked the beginning of the end for the prominent position held by that Church in western Europe apart from Ireland, Scotland and Wales. In Ireland especially, however, the seemingly vanquished actually were victorious, for the *Hibernenses*, as Kathleen Hughes observes, 'triumphed'. They may have lost the battle over the dating of Easter, the shape of the tonsure, episcopal ordination and (maybe) the rite of baptism, but in the long run they won the war 'not to bring the Church into line with continental practice, but to adjust it to the native law' . The Irish Church retained its semi-autonomous character. In fact its idiosyncrasy was increased, for, by the end of the eighth century with the destruction of the diocesan system under pressure from the Vikings, it had become a totally monastic institution.

Although political ambition and self-interest may have been upper-most in the minds of some of the protagonists, Whitby was basically an argument about papal authority and local autonomy; about the need for universally-accepted church practices and the possibility of allowing usages peculiar to individual Churches. It is a milestone in the history of the Church: the triumph of uniformity, ecclesiastical discipline, good sense and, ultimately, Christian charity over eccentricity, factionalism and obscurantism. After four-and-a-half centuries, the decree of the Council of Arles (314) that Easter should be observed *uno die et uno tempore per omnem orbem* ('by all throughout the world on the one day, at the same time') had been put into effect. Whitby also brought about standardisation regarding the administration of the sacraments of holy orders and (perhaps) baptism. Yet the Easter controversy did not end the independence of the two-hundred-year-old Irish Church; the Celtic Church ultimately was to achieve the victory of legitimate localism over sterile centralism. The aftermath of Whitby was a triumph both for uniformity and for diversity.

Notes:

1. We are fortunate in modern English to be able to use two words, *Easter* and *Pasch*, to refer to our holiest festival. These terms come from two very different backgrounds and give us two very different but valid perceptions of 'the Feast of Feasts'. Our word *Easter*, with its roots in Old English, has pagan origins. The Anglo-Saxon *Eastre* possibly enshrines the name of their dawn-goddess *Eostre*. It is closely related to the Old English *eastan*, the Dutch *oost* and the German *Osten*, all meaning 'east' and all coming originally from the Old Teutonic word for 'east' or 'dawn'. Easter, then, is packed with suggestions about hope, light, regeneration and new life. Its root in the word for 'east' or 'dawn' reminds us that in Christ's resurrection the sun rose upon us. The Romance languages and Celtic

tongues like Irish and Welsh, however, are truer to Judaeo-Christian traditions in their use of words to describe this holy season. The Irish, Welsh, French and Spanish words *Cáisc, y-Pasg, Pâques* and *Pascuas*, for instance, come indirectly through Latin (*Pascha*) and Greek (*Paskha*). These, in turn, are derived from the Hebrew term *Pesakh*, the 'Passover', the Jewish commemoration of their deliverance from death and emancipation from slavery in Egypt to life and freedom in the Promised Land. (The Irish term, of course, reflects the adoption by some of the Celtic languages of the Q sound for the P one.)

2. Monsignor P J Corish [1971] believes that attendance at Sunday Mass and servile work on the Sabbath were also discussed at Whitby. This is a distinct possibility. Corish notes that Sunday observance is referred to in Muirchú and Adomnan. He says that these works date from the century after 'the suspension of labour on Sunday seems to have made its appearance in Europe.'

3. Alfred P Smyth suggests that Oswiu's authority in the principality of Deira, where his son was in control, could have been totally undermined by his adherence to the Celtic practices. The King's ambitions outside his own territory, south of the Humber and north of the Forth, could have been similarly affected. Oswiu also had to contend with the incipient nationalism of the young English Church which had begun to chafe at its continuing subordination to Iona and the Irish Church. King Oswiu had, therefore, to neutralise the party which posed the greatest threat to his own power-base. In this case it meant siding with them. Smyth claims that 'the real issues at Whitby were primarily political while arguments about the date of Easter and set speeches on Saint Peter were little more than a smoke-screen to hide more pressing issues'.

CHAPTER TWELVE

Celtic Church Art

*'... an island rich in goods,
jewels, cloth, and gold ...'*

[From a Hiberno-Latin poem
by Donatus, c 829-887]

A present-day visitor to the National Museum of Ireland, which houses a large portion of the country's early Christian relics, cannot fail to be impressed by the variety and richness of these artifacts. Even to the untrained eye there is no doubting the skill and creativity of Irish Christian artists and craftsmen in the first centuries of Christianity in the country. But their work was not produced in a vacuum; a debt, the extent of which is difficult to assess, is owed to the skilled and gifted men who laboured in Ireland before the coming of Christianity.

One of the most impressive survivals from Stone Age Ireland is the megalithic tumulus at Newgrange on the River Boyne. A large carved stone at the entrance to this tomb displays an intricate pattern of spirals. Geometric decorations are to be found on other megaliths at the base of the tomb. Little else of artistic merit has survived from this very early period.

At some time after 400BC the migrating Hallstatt Celts began to arrive in Ireland. They were followed by the La Tène Celts who settled in the country between 150-100BC and who had a seminal influence on the development of Celtic art. They were fascinated by rich ornaments,

136

like torcs or neck-rings of gold or bronze, which they used for personal adornment. An example of these is the richly decorated collar found at Broighter, Co Derry and dated to the first century BC. This torc is only part of what is known as the Broighter gold hoard, unearthed by a labourer named Tom Nicholl on the farm of Joseph Gibson near Limavady in February 1896. The treasure was sold by Mr Gibson for a derisory few sovereigns to a jeweller in Derry. The hoard was later acquired by the British Museum for six hundred pounds. After a celebrated law-case it found its way to the Royal Irish Academy in Dublin as treasure-trove. It is now on display in the National Museum and replicas can be seen in Belfast's Ulster Museum. The principal motifs on this gold collar are s-shaped scrolls incorporating slender trumpets and terminating in leaf-shapes. Small discs, formed like snail-shells, are another prominent feature.

From an even earlier period are the six bronze scabbards which were also found in the north of Ireland, at Lisnacroghera, Toomebridge, Co Antrim and Coleraine, Co Derry. Finely decorated, they are examples of the skill and precision of the Celtic craftsmen. The inclusion of spirals in the designs of these various treasures from the north of Ireland shows a contact with the aboriginal stone-carving. But the La Tène Celts were also innovative: to enhance their decoration they used the technique of enamelling. This can be seen on another bronze object from Lisnacroghera (two tiny ducks on a red enamel plate) and more explicitly on a small, enamelled bronze disc, dating from the first century AD, unearthed at Somerset, near Ballinasloe, Co Galway. The latter is of great importance because, as Françoise Henry [1965] explains, the process of enamelling used in this case is almost identical to that used on the bosses of the Ardagh Chalice centuries later. This shows the continuity between the techniques of pagan and Christian artificers.

Although it was removed from the immediate sphere of Roman influence, a number of new techniques reached Ireland from the empire. One of these was the Gallo-Roman development of combining segments of millefiori glass with the former process of champlevé whereby coloured paste was set in depressions or furrows cast or cut on metal. This new approach is to be seen to great effect in the penannular brooches, a most splendid and popular form of Celtic artistic expression. Another innovation was filigree work, the delicate soldering together of gold or silver wire, sometimes to a solid back, to produce a lacework effect.

The Celts also displayed their artistry on large, unshaped stones. Examples of these are to be found on Boa Island, Co Fermanagh (see page 33), Turoe, Co Galway and Castlestrange, Co Roscommon. The two specimens in Connacht are decorated with curvilinear motifs, typical of the continental Celts. They are among the finest examples in Europe of what was probably a series of ritual stones decorated with Celtic ornament.

Pre-Christian art in Ireland developed a degree of individuality. The La Tène craftsmen were able to flourish in an area far-removed from Roman influences. Above all, their art is known for its complex but fluid symmetry. Expert use of the compass (for example, in the Somerset hoard or in the displays on the bone slips from Lough Crew) gives attractive reality to abstract ideas. It is from these roots that the superb productions of the Christian era were to stem.

With the development of Christianity in Ireland and the invigorating adoption of the monastic way of life, Celtic artistic endeavour became centred on the monasteries. These gradually became great centres of study as well as worship. Learning was not, of course, seen as an end in itself but as a means of knowing and worshipping Christ more fully. Similarly, art flourished as a powerful expression of devotion, and stone slabs, chalices, sacred books and other items were crafted by artists to be edifying aids to the community's adoration of God. The beautiful objects which these men produced were remotely indebted to some of our earliest ancestors, like the Stone Age builders of Newgrange. They were richly influenced by the dominant Celtic culture of the later settlers. But just as Christianity reached Ireland by various means, so too art in Ireland was influenced by ideas from abroad: from Britain, the mainland Roman empire, north Africa and the near East.

The stone crosses, which are still quite numerous and remarkably well preserved in various parts of the country, bear testimony to the developing skill of the artists in the early Christian period. Initially, unshaped pillars or large slab stones were decorated with lines and spirals, reminiscent of work in the pre-Christian era, and had as their centre of attention a simple Latin or Greek cross (for example, the Reask Pillar in Co Kerry on page 105). Gradually the workmanship on these large stones became more and more developed. The upright slabs were given a cruciform shape and human figures were introduced. These innovations can be found on two crosses in Co Donegal, one at Fahan(see page 115) and the other at Carndonagh (see page 131), both dated as seventh century. The emerging arms on Saint Mura's Cross at Fahan show the first tentative steps in the making of cruciform slabs. The Carndonagh Stele is more obviously cross-shaped. Both of these monuments would probably have been painted to highlight their decoration which involves incised interlacing. Two figures are displayed on the front of the Fahan Cross (page 115 shows the back of the cross) and it bears an inscription in Greek, giving a version of the *Gloria Patri* formula in use since the fourth Council of Toledo [633]. The Carndonagh Cross, standing more than ten feet in height, is an impressive monument and marks a definite break with the unshaped slab.

By the end of the eighth century the crosses began to take on a more pronounced cruciform shape, with the arms and the characteristic open ring becoming the principal features. The Crosses at Ahenny, decorated in a fashion similar to the *Book of Kells*, are particularly fine examples. The manuscript and these monuments are generally regarded as being contemporaneous. In the ninth century, sculptors began to carve scenes which depicted events in the Bible on the crosses but it was not until the tenth century that this particular art-form reached its zenith with the creation of the magnificent High Crosses, such as the Cross of Muiredach at Monasterboice, Co Louth, one of the finest examples in the country. These High Crosses, with their elaborately carved scenes from sacred scripture, are Bibles in stone, which onlookers from different educational backgrounds, and with different devotional interests, would seek.

Much of what remains of the metalwork of our period is secular rather than religious in purpose. The Vikings, whose first recorded raid on Ireland took place in 795, would seem to have been particularly attracted to the highly ornate metal objects produced in great quantities in the secular workshops and in monasteries. Many of the relics which escaped this spoliation are remarkably beautiful and most skilfully crafted. We can only feel a great sense of frustration at what has been lost. The Christian craftsmen produced metal objects in bronze, often plated with either gold or silver. They profited from the rich inheritance passed on to them by the early Celts and used their very sophisticated techniques to produce objects of relatively straightforward design with a proliferation of simple spirals and whorls.

They employed the techniques of champlevé, millefiori and filigree work. Champlevé, of course, was a skill brought from Europe by the Celts in pagan times. When this method was combined with that of millefiori – literally meaning 'one thousand flowers' – a rich, sparkling effect was achieved. Filigree work was another skill which had been known and used by metal-workers in early Celtic Ireland. It was, no doubt, because of the plundering of the monasteries by the

Norsemen that mainly non-ecclesiastical articles have survived. Examples of these are penannular brooches and pins. Very fine filigree work can be seen in the decoration of the small gold bird found at Garryduff, Co Cork, dating from the second half of the seventh century. These techniques were further refined and developed until in the eighth century they were employed with total mastery in the production of the Tara (pseudopenannular) Brooch and, above all, in the creation of the Ardagh Chalice and the Derrynaflan Paten.

Michael Ryan [1983] has described the Ardagh Chalice as 'perhaps the finest Irish work in metal from the first millennium AD.' Inspired by Byzantine sixth-century prototypes, the decoration and workmanship show that the sacred vessel is of Irish manufacture. It adapts local (scrolls and interlace, for instance) and foreign (Germanic animal ornament, for example) traditions of decoration, and techniques of design (like filigree, enamelling and casting) to the production of a liturgical vessel. The chalice is sumptuously decorated in places but, as G Frank Mitchell remarks, 'the designer did not hesitate to reserve large areas from decoration just as the artists of the *Book of Durrow* set their design off against pure vellum.' The lettering on the chalice is reminiscent of the script used in the *Lindisfarne Gospels* and the combination of designs on the flange at the base of the cup is remarkably similar to a section of the *Chi-Rho* page in the *Book of Kells*. Etienne Rynne dates the Ardagh Chalice to the period c 710-735. The chalice was discovered accidentally, in 1868, by a man named Quinn who was digging potatoes in an ancient ring-fort on his farm at Ardagh, Co Limerick. The find was presented to the Royal Irish Academy in 1878 and the chalice is now in the National Museum.

The Derrynaflan Paten is the most significant piece in a hoard of treasure – a chalice, a wine-strainer, the large circular paten and a bronze bowl – found by an Englishman called Michael Webb and his teenage son in February 1980 at the site of Saint Ruadán's Monastery in the townland of Derrynaflan, Killenaule, Co Tipperary {Note 1}. The Webbs were using metal detectors. Recently the Irish Supreme Court determined that the treasure belongs to the state. The hoard has been estimated (notionally) to be worth more than five million Irish pounds. Restored in London, the artifacts from Derrynaflan are now on display in the National Museum in Dublin. A large array of letters on the paten suggest that it was crafted in a scholarly milieu, presumably a monastery. Some of its borrowings lead experts to the conclusion that it dates from the ninth century. Its most striking ornamental feature is the series of twenty-four filigree panels which contain animal representations, interlace and curvilinear motifs.

Cross of Muiredach at Monasterboice, Co Louth
Photo: courtesy Office of Public Works, Dublin

It should be no surprise that manuscripts were frequently used as sources of inspiration by the metal-workers, for the Irish monks spent part of their day in studying and copying the sacred scriptures. Legend has it that Colum Cille was guilty of making a copy of a psalter belonging to Saint Finnian. Some regard the *Cathach* as being that copy. Probably dating from the time of Colum Cille, it is the oldest surviving Irish manuscript. It has had a chequered career. It was the prized possession of the O'Donnells of Co Donegal, collateral descendants of Colum Cille himself, and was taken by them, as a mascot, into their numerous battles. After the Flight of the Earls (1607), it saw service with the O'Donnells on the battlefields of Europe for almost two hundred years before being returned to Ireland at the start of the nineteenth century. This may help to explain why it has been rather badly preserved and is incomplete.

The book, originally measuring about 150 mm x 230 mm, is written in an early, but fully developed, form of the Irish majuscule. It is simply decorated. Each psalm begins with a large capital letter, the succeeding letters of the first word becoming smaller until they merge into the main text. The initial characters are painted in brown ink and are normally outlined in red and yellow. Many of them are surrounded by lines of red dots (perhaps showing Coptic influence) and are adorned by La Tène pelta, scroll and trumpet designs. These decorations also appear on the metal artifacts – latchets, hand-pins and penannular brooches - being produced in Ireland at the same time. Occasional fish motifs and tiny crosses in the book are obviously of early Christian inspiration. The *Cathach* can be viewed, by arrangement, at the Royal Irish Academy, Dublin.

An examination of works associated with Columban's monastery of Bobbio, in the decades immediately after his death in 615, shows the growing complexity of the decoration in Irish manuscripts. Many of these – some probably of an Irish provenance – are now housed in the Ambrosian Library in Milan. They retain familiar Celtic features, particularly of script, and contrast starkly with Italian works of the period. The most novel characteristic of these Bobbio manuscripts, and especially of the *Codex Ambrosianus* D. 23, is the decorative page which appears at the beginning of each section of a book. Coptic in origin, this carpet-page, as it is termed, is given over completely to embellishment.

But it is the *Book of Durrow* which marks one of the first high points of Irish manuscript production in the early Christian period. Where and when this earliest of the 'prestige' manuscripts was copied and illuminated is not known but many authorities are drawn towards a

Northumbrian or Ionan origin and an early-to-mid-seventh-century dating {Note 2}. It is known that it was at Durrow from the Middle Ages until the dissolution of the monastery at the Reformation. The book then found itself in the hands of a local farmer. Superstitious and not a bibliophile, this good man used to dip it in buckets of water to drench his cattle! In the second half of the seventeenth century it was acquired by Henry Jones, Anglican bishop of Meath, and presented to the Library of Trinity College, Dublin.

The book contains the Vulgate version of the four Gospels, canon tables, Saint Jerome's letter to Pope Damasus, prefaces, summaries of the text, and glossaries. It has two hundred and forty-eight rather small leaves (each 245 mm x 745 mm in size). The script is a refined form of the Irish majuscule. At the beginning of each Gospel is a page illustrating the symbol of an evangelist but these symbols do not correspond with the Gospels which they precede. The symbols are in the order of the Old Latin version of the Gospels while the text follows the order in the Vulgate. Three of the Gospels in the *Book of Durrow* are also preceded by carpet-pages. Matthew's Gospel has no such introduction; the carpet-page before Saint Jerome's letter has obviously been put in the wrong place in a rebinding of the work. The introductory words of each Gospel are ornamented. Four colours are used in the book: brownish-black, brilliant red, yellow and green. Modern authorities, like Gunther Haseloff and Uta Roth, have pointed out that the use of the red and yellow colours and the chequered design, suggestive of millefiori enamelling, used by the artist in the symbol of the evangelist just before Matthew's Gospel, show the links between the manuscript illuminator and the metalworker in the early Middle Ages.

The main designs are spirals and broad-ribbon interlacing rather similar to those used on the Fahan and Carndonagh Crosses and on the Gospel-fragment (manuscript A. II. 10) in Durham Cathedral Library. This interlace probably has Mediterranean – possibly Coptic – roots. Another interesting characteristic of the book is the animal ornament to be found on one of the carpet-pages (folio 192b). In this page the artist presents six different panels, each of them containing strange little interwoven creatures. This animal ornament was unknown in late Celtic art but is a feature of Anglo-Saxon metalwork. The *Book of Durrow* shows the eclectic nature of seventh-century Irish art. Three influences went into its production: (1) native Irish; (2) Mediterranean (possibly Coptic); and (3) Anglo-Saxon or Germanic {Note 3}. Overall the *Book of Durrow* marks a mid-point in the development of Irish manuscript-production. Although infinitely more sophisticated than the *Cathach*, it retains, nevertheless, a oneness with the earlier work and lacks the precision, skill, assimilation of different influences and spirit of adventure which distinguish the great manuscripts of the eighth and ninth centuries.

Two other significant manuscripts from this stage of partial development in Irish scribal activity have survived. They are the *Lindisfarne Gospels* and the *Lichfield Gospels*, both produced in Great Britain but obviously under Irish influence. These two works reveal further developments in calligraphy. They are also noteworthy for their frequent use of animal interlacing. The *Lindisfarne Gospels*, probably the work of Eadfrith, bishop of Lindisfarne from 698 - 721, is more elaborate, complex and colourful than the *Book of Durrow*. Françoise Henry (1965), however, suggests that the book is 'handled with a certain amount of stiffness very different from the imaginative treatment of the painter of the Book of Durrow.' *Lindisfarne* is noted for the brilliance of its colours, a radiance achieved by frequently using together different tones of the same colour. The *Lichfield Gospels*, an eighth-century work thought to be of Welsh origin, is much closer to the authentic spirit of Irish art. Its method of covering ink of one colour with a light wash of another pigment is innovative; a technique to be used again, to supreme effect, in the illumination of the *Book of Kells*.

The *Book of Kells* is the most magnificent of the insular scriptural manuscripts; with it the pinnacle was reached in scribal work. It dates from the late eighth or early ninth century. With a recorded history from 1007 in the Columban house at Kells, the manuscript was probably not penned or illuminated in the Co Meath monastery. Iona is its most likely place of origin. Scholars think that the incomplete manuscript was taken from there to Kells towards the end of the first decade of the ninth century to preserve it from Viking marauders. It remained in Kells, in the monastery and, following the Reformation, in the parish church, from about 910 until 1654 when it was brought to Dublin for safe-keeping during the Cromwellian period. Bishop Henry Jones donated it to Trinity College, Dublin, later in the same century.

It is made up of the four Gospels, a number of prefaces, resumés of the text, canon-tables and some twelfth-century records (in Irish) of the monastery of Kells. The Vulgate edition of the Gospels is chiefly used but the narrative is interspersed with extracts from the Old Latin version. Penned in majuscule script, the book has three hundred and forty leaves, (each of them 330 mm x 250 mm in dimension). At least three artists co-operated in its ornamentation. The range and opulence of its colours, the extent and variety of its elaboration, and

Matthew, from the Book of Durrow
Photo: courtesy Trinity College, Dublin

the sheer mastery of the artists who illuminated it make the *Book of Kells* a priceless work of art and the supreme production of the Irish artistic milieu of that time.

A mention of the *Book of Kells* is a fitting conclusion to this short history of the early Celtic Church. This great manuscript is a noble symbol of a mighty institution. It is itself a most beautiful creation. But it is more than a thing of beauty. To view it simply as an *objet d'art* is to do it – and all the religious objects emanating from the Celtic Church – a gross injustice. *Kells* and the other relics are the product of a vital and individual Church and mirror the organisation which produced them. Religious inspiration begets art. Behind the technique and the craftsmanship is belief. The Irish sculptors, calligraphers and metalworkers were masters of their specific arts but none of their productions is entirely spontaneous; their artistry is conscious, sophisticated and unaccidental. What they did, they did on purpose. This is not to belittle them, for the true artist is a conscious creator. The artists of the early Irish Church knew exactly what they wished to depict and achieve. They did this with genuineness and authenticity and – most importantly – faith.

The Celtic Church was, as the late Donnchadh Ó Floinn pointed out, grounded in 'the sources of revelation'; having a profound awareness of 'communion with the Body of Christ at prayer'; and with 'a deep sense of its own continuity'. Perhaps we are not fair to the late scholar when we view the chief characteristics of the early Irish Church as 'scriptural'; 'ecclesial'; and 'sanctoral'. These words limit the insights of An tAthair Ó Floinn. Nevertheless, they are useful pointers to highlight the main features of the relics of the early Irish Church. That Church was strikingly conscious of being based on sacred scripture (*scriptural*) and tradition. Its members were acutely aware of being a community of faith, parts of the Church, the Body of Christ (*ecclesial*). It had a keen sense of its origins, continuity and future; of what used to be called the Church Triumphant, the Church Militant and the Church Suffering (*sanctoral*).

The sculptured crosses are Bibles in stone. In their peculiar medium they reflect the scripture-based nature of Irish Christianity (*scriptural*). They acknowledge and revere Christ who died on the Cross, of course, but they are not sombre statements about suffering and death. They are joyful, triumphant expressions, celebrating, above all, the Church which flows from Christ's sacrificial death. It is no coincidence that there is a striking dependence on John's Gospel in the decoration of the great Celtic crosses. Johannine theology is heavily ecclesial in content. John links Christ's giving up of the spirit

Matthew, detail from The Book of Kells
Photo: courtesy Trinity College, Dublin

on Calvary with his gift of the Holy Spirit at Pentecost, the beginning of the Church. For the Irish sculptors the stone cross symbolised the birth of the Church accomplished by the glorified, reigning King (*ecclesial*). Many of the stone crosses – even the primitive Carndonagh Stele with its three human figures – have depictions of saints, bishops and laity (*sanctoral*).

The biblical manuscripts, with their reverence for the sacred text, also concentrate on the 'scriptural', 'ecclesial' and 'sanctoral'. They are elegant, awe-filled presentations of God's word. They are typical of a Christianity that, since the time of Patrick, had been steeped in sacred scripture (*scriptural*) and also in the tradition of the Church. Again the communal emphasis of Celtic Christianity can be seen in these books. We take two relatively unknown manuscripts to illustrate this point. The representations of the crucifixion in the Codex A. II. 17 in the Cathedral Library in Durham and in the *Saint Gall Gospels* in the Cathedral Library in St Gall, Switzerland, depict the death of the Saviour as recorded by Saint John. At the foot of the cross stand two soldiers, one with the sponge and one with the lance. This recalls both Christ's death and the birth of the Church: from the Lord's side flowed blood and water – his death led to redemption and entrance, through the waters of baptism, into the Church (*ecclesial*). The *Book of Kells* is filled with illustrations of members of the Church both heroic and ordinary. Another feature is the representation of another world, somewhat surreal, and filled with animal forms which suggest by their ambivalence a link between the two worlds – earth and heaven (*sanctoral*).

The Ardagh Chalice and the Derrynaflan Paten are undoubtedly glorious liturgical receptacles but they are such in order to be suitable vessels for their sacred function. In some of their decoration they link the worshipper to his scriptural roots. The Ardagh Chalice has an inscription in Latin listing the names of eleven of the original apostles and Saint Paul (*scriptural, ecclesial* and *sanctoral*). These sacred vessels are as worthy as their artificers could make them of the function they were crafted to perform. They were made to hold the body and blood of the Lord so that the 'Body of Christ', the Church, might be fed and nourished.

When Patrick came to Ireland, the country was considered a heathen backwater at the ends of the earth. Its infant Church was of almost no significance in the eyes of most Europeans. By the end of the seventh century, Ireland was a vital and influential society, respected throughout the western world which it had enriched. As it reached maturity, the Celtic Church produced many precious artifacts. Although splendid, they are merely the physical representations of a spiritual reality. These relics typify the adult Irish Church – glorious and confident, subtle and sophisticated, cosmopolitan and individual, edifying and inspiring, but, above all, Christ-centred.

Notes:

1. Ruadán was, of course, one of the so-called 'Twelve Apostles of Ireland'.

2. In a recent publication, however, Dáibhí Ó Cróinín argues that the manuscript was produced in an Irish environment, in the monastery of Rath Melsigi, which 'would have housed a mixed community of Anglo-Saxons, Irish, and perhaps even Franks.'

3. In *Celtic Britain and Ireland, AD 200-800: The Myth of the Dark Ages* (Blackrock, Co Dublin, 1990), Lloyd and Jennifer Laing reconsider a number of traditionally accepted views regarding the influences exercised from outside on Irish artistic effort. They state, for instance, that 'the case for Coptic influence in Irish art is not strong.'

BIBLIOGRAPHY AND REFERENCES

This long bibliography is included to assist enthusiasts in their studies. Only some of the books listed here have been referred to above. Where there is more than one work by an individual author for a specific chapter in this reading list, references in the text are by date of publication.

General Studies

Bieler, L., *Ireland: Harbinger of the Middle Ages* (Oxford, 1963).

De Paor, L., *Saint Patrick's World* (Blackrock, Co Dublin, 1993).

De Paor, M. and L., *Early Christian Ireland* (London, 1958).

Hughes, K., *The Church in Early Irish Society* (London, 1966).

Hughes, K., *Early Christian Ireland: Introduction to the Sources* (London, 1972).

Hughes, K. and Hamlin, A., *The Modern Traveller to the Early Irish Church* (London, 1977).

Kenney, J.F., *The Sources for the Early History of Ireland, Ecclesiastical: An Introduction and Guide* (New York, 1929; reprinted with additions by L. Bieler, Shannon, 1968; reissued Dublin, 1979).

Mac Niocaill, G., *Ireland before the Vikings* (Dublin and London, 1972).

Mc Neill, J. T., *The Celtic Churches* (Chicago, 1974).

Moody, T.W. and Martin, F.X. (eds), *The Course of Irish History* (Cork, 1967).

Ó Corrain, D., 'A Handlist of Publications on Early Irish History' in *Historical Studies* 10 (1976); pp 172-203.

Richter, M., *Medieval Ireland: The Enduring Tradition* (Dublin, 1988).

Chapter One: Pre-Patrician Christianity

Bieler, L., 'St Patrick and the Coming of Christianity' in Corish, P.J. (ed), *A History of Irish Catholicism*, vol. 1, fasc. 1 (Dublin, 1967).

Bieler, L. (ed. and trans.), *The Patrician Texts in the Book of Armagh* (Dublin, 1979).

Bowen, E.G., Saints, *Seaways and Settlements in the Celtic Lands* (Cardiff, 1969).

Carney, J., *The Problem of St Patrick* (Dublin, 1961).

Corish, P.J., *The Irish Catholic Experience: A Historical Survey* (Dublin, 1985).

De Paor, L., *Saint Patrick's World* (Blackrock, Co Dublin, 1993).

De Paor, L.,'The Coming of Christianity' in De Paor, L (ed.), *Milestones in Irish History* (Cork and Dublin, 1986); pp 20-30.

Gildas. Winterbottom, M. (ed. and trans.), *Gildas. The Ruin of Britain and other works* (Chichester, 1978).

Giraldus Cambrensis. O'Meara, J.J. (ed. and trans.), *Gerald of Wales: The History and Topography of Ireland* (London, 1982).

Herren, M. (ed. and trans.), *The Hisperica Famina I. The A-Text: a new critical edition with translation and philological commentary* (Toronto, 1974).

Kenney, J.F., *The Sources for the Early History of Ireland, Ecclesiastical: an Introduction and Guide* (New York, 1929; reprinted with additions by L. Bieler, Shannon, 1968; reissued Dublin, 1979).

Ó Fiaich, T., 'The Beginnings of Christianity' in Moody, T.W., and Martin, F.X. (eds), *The Course of Irish History* (Cork, 1967); pp 61-75.

O'Rahilly, T.F., *The Two Patricks: a Lecture on the History of Christianity in Fifth-Century Ireland* (Dublin, 1942).

Orosius. Zangemeister, C. (ed.), *Historiarum adversum paganos,* 1 (7 vols. Leipzig, 1875-1906).

Prosper of Aquitaine, 'Epitoma Chronicon' in Migne, J.P. (ed.) *Patrologia Latina,* 51 (221 vols. Paris, 1844-64); col. 269-270.

Prosper of Aquitaine, 'Contra Collatorem' in Migne, J.P. (ed.) *Patrologia Latina,* 51 (221 vols. Paris, 1844-64); col. 599.

Ryan, J., *Irish Monasticism: Origins and Early Development* (London, 1931; reissued New York, 1972).

Ryan, J., 'The Traditional View' in Ryan, J. (ed), *Saint Patrick* (Dublin, 1958); pp 10-23.

Tacitus. Ogilvie, R. M. and Richmond, I. (eds), *Cornelii Taciti; De Vita Agricolae* (Oxford, 1967).

Thomas, C., *Celtic Britain* (London, 1986).

Thompson, E.A., *Who was Saint Patrick?* (Woodbridge, Suffolk, 1985).

Chapter Two: Patrick: The Man

Bieler, L. (ed.), *Libri epistolarum Sancti Patricii Episcopi* (2 vols; Dublin, 1952).

Bieler, L., 'St Patrick and the Coming of Christianity' in Corish, P.J. (ed.), *A History of Irish Catholicism,* vol.1, fasc. 1 (Dublin, 1967).

Bieler, L., *The Life and Legend of St Patrick: Problems of Modern Scholarship* (Dublin, 1949).

Bieler, L. (ed. and trans.), *The Irish Penitentials* (Dublin, 1963; second edition, 1975).

Bieler, L. (ed. and trans.), *The Patrician Texts in the Book of Armagh* (Dublin, 1979).

Bieler, L., 'The Problem of "Silva Focluti"' in *Irish Historical Studies,* 3 (1942-3); pp 351-64.

Binchy, D.A., 'Patrick and his Biographers: Ancient and Modern' in *Studia Hibernica,* 2 (1962); pp 7-173.

Binchy, D.A., 'Saint Patrick's "First Synod"' in *Studia Hibernica,* 9 (1968) pp 49-59.

Bury, J.B., *The life of St Patrick and his place in History* (London, 1905).

Carney, J., *The Problem of St Patrick* (Dublin, 1961).

Conneely, D., *The Letters of Saint Patrick* (Maynooth, 1993).

Concannon, H., *Saint Patrick: His Life and Mission* (Dublin, 1931).

Corish, P.J., *The Irish Catholic Experience: A Historical Survey* (Dublin, 1985).

De Breffny, B., *In the Steps of St Patrick* (London, 1982).

De Paor, L., *Saint Patrick's World* (Blackrock, Co Dublin, 1993)

Duffy, J. (ed. and trans.), *Patrick in his own Words* (Dublin, 1975).

Esposito, M., 'The Patrician Problem and a Possible Solution' in *Irish Historical Studies* 10, (1956); pp 131-55.

Esposito, M., 'The Problem of the Two Patricks' in Ryan, J. (ed.), *Saint Patrick* (Dublin, 1958); pp 38-52.

Hanson, R.P.C., *Saint Patrick: His Origins and Career* (Oxford, 1968).

Hanson, R.P.C., *The Life and Writings of the Historical Saint Patrick* (New York, 1983).

Howlett, D., *'Ex Saliva Scripturae Mea'* in O Corráin, D., Breathnach, L. and McCone, K. (eds.), *Sages, saints and storytellers: Celtic studies in honour of Professor James Carney* (Maynooth, 1989); pp 86-101.

Hughes, K., *The Church in Early Irish Society* (London, 1966).

Hughes, K., *Early Christian Ireland: Introduction to the Sources* (London, 1972).

Jackson, K., *Language and History in Early Britain* (Edinburgh, 1953).

Kenney, J.F., *The sources for the Early History of Ireland, Ecclesiastical: An Introduction and Guide* (New York, 1929; reprinted with additions by L. Bieler, Shannon, 1968; reissued Dublin, 1969).

Mac Neill, E., *St Patrick: Apostle of Ireland* (London, 1934).

Mac Neill, E., 'Silva Focluti' in *Proceedings of the Royal Irish Academy*, 36, sect. C (1923); pp 249-55.

Mc Erlean, J., 'Silva Focluti' in *Analecta Bollandiana*, 57 (1939) pp 334-63. See Larkin, A.J. (trans.), 'Rev. John Mc Erlean on Silva Focluti' in *Journal of the South Derry Historical Society*, I. 3 (1982-3); pp 225-42.

Mohrmann, C., *The Latin of Saint Patrick: Four Lectures* (Dublin, 1961).

Morris, H., 'The Wood of Foclut: Silva Focluti' in *Journal of the Down and Connor Historical Society*, 8 (1937); pp 5-16.

Morris, J., 'Introduction' to Hood, A.E.B. (ed. and trans.), *St Patrick: His Writings and Muirchu's Life* (London and Chichester, 1978).

O'Donoghue, N.D., *Aristocracy of Soul: Patrick of Ireland* (Wilmington, Delaware, 1987).

O'Rahilly, T.F., *The Two Patricks: A Lecture on the History of Christianity in Fifth-Century Ireland* (Dublin, 1942).

Patrick (?). 'Lorica' in Todd, J.H., *St Patrick, Apostle of Ireland: A Memoir of his Life and Mission* (Dublin, 1864).

Shaw, F., *The Real St Patrick* (Dublin, 1931).

Thompson, E. A., *Who was Saint Patrick?* (Woodbridge, Suffolk, 1985).

Chapter Three: Patrick: The Mission and its Setting

Adamson, I., *The Cruthin: A History of the Ulster Land and People* (Belfast, 1974).

Bieler, L. (ed.), *Libri epistolarum Sancti Patricii Episcopi* (2 vols; Dublin, 1952).

Bieler, L., 'St Patrick and the Coming of Christianity' in Corish, P.J.(ed.), *A History of Irish Catholicism*, vol. 1, fasc. 1 (Dublin, 1967).

Bord, J. and C., *Early Rites: Fertility Practices in Pre-Industrial Britain* (St Albans, 1983).

Byrne, F.J., 'Early Irish Society' in Moody, T.W. and Martin, F.X. (eds.) *The Course of Irish History* (Cork, 1967); pp 43-60.

Byrne, F.J., *Irish Kings and High Kings* (London, 1973).

Chadwick, N.K., *The Celts* (London, 1970).

Colum Cille (?), 'Lorica' in Best, R.I. (ed.), *Martyrology of Tallagh* (London, 1931).

Conneely, D., *The Letters of Saint Patrick* (Maynooth, 1993).

Delaney, F., *The Celts* (London, 1986).

De Paor, L., *Saint Patrick's World* (Blackrock, Co Dublin, 1993).

Dillon, M. and Chadwick, N., *The Celtic Realms* (London, 1967).

Giraldus Cambrensis. O'Meara, J.J. (ed. and trans.), *Gerald of Wales: The History and Topography of Ireland* (London, 1982).

Green, M., *Symbol and Image in Celtic Religious Art* (London, 1990).

Kelly, F., *A Guide to Early Irish Law* (Dublin,1988).

Laing, L. and J., *Celtic Britain And Ireland, AD 200-800: The Myth of the Dark Ages* (Blackrock, Co Dublin, 1990).

Mac Niocaill, G., *Ireland before the Vikings* (Dublin and London, 1972).

Ó Corráin, D., 'Women in early Irish society' in Mac Curtain, M. and Ó Corráin, D. (eds), *Women in Irish Society* (Dublin, 1978); pp 1-13.

Ó Fiaich, T., 'The Celts I', in Loughrey, P. (ed.), *The People of Ireland* (Belfast, 1988); pp26-39.

O'Riordain, S.P., *Antiquities of the Irish Countryside* (London, 1942).

Ross, A., *Pagan Celtic Britain* (London, 1974).

Chapter Four: Patrick and the Church of Armagh

Adamson, I., 'Selected Translations from the Bangor Antiphonary' in *Bangor: Light of the World* (Bangor, 1979); pp 197-211.

Bede. Colgrove, B. and Mynors, R.A.B. (eds and trans.), *Bede's Ecclesiastical History of the English People* (Oxford, 1969).

Bieler, L. (ed. and trans.), *The Patrician Texts in the Book of Armagh* (Dublin, 1979).

Binchy, D.A., 'Patrick and his Biographers: Ancient and Modern' in *Studia Hibernica*, 2 (1962); pp 7-173.

Byrne, F.J., *Irish Kings and High Kings* (London, 1973).

Carney, J., *The Problem of St Patrick* (Dublin, 1961).

Corish, P.J., 'The Christian Mission' in Corish, P.J. (ed.), *A History of Irish Catholicism, vol. 1, fasc. 3 (Dublin, 1972).

De Paor, L., *Saint Patrick's World* (Blackrock, Co Dublin, 1993).

De Paor, L., 'The Aggrandisement of Armagh' in *Historical Studies*, 8 (1971); pp 95-110.

Gwynn, J. (ed.), *The Book of Armagh* (Dublin and London, 1913).

Hamlin, A. (ed.), *Historical Monuments of Northern Ireland* (Belfast, 1983).

Harbison, P., *Pre-Christian Ireland: From the First Settlers to the Early Celts* (London, 1988).

Hood, A.E.B. (ed. and trans.), *St Patrick: His Writings and Muirchu's Life* (London and Chichester, 1978).

Hughes, K., *The Church in Early Irish Society* (London, 1966).

Hughes, K., *Early Christian Ireland: Introduction to the Sources* (London, 1972).

Mac Airt, S. and Mac Niocaill, G. (eds and trans.), *The Annals of Ulster* (Dublin, 1983).

Mac Neill, E., *St Patrick: Apostle of Ireland* (London, 1934).

Mac Niocaill, G., *Ireland before the Vikings* (Dublin and London, 1972).

McCone, K., 'An Introduction to Early Irish Saints' Lives' in *The Maynooth Review*, 11 (1984); pp 26-59.

Mallory, J.P., *Navan Fort: The Ancient Capital of Ulster* (Belfast, 1985).

Ó Fiaich, T., 'St Patrick and Armagh' in *Irish Ecclesiastical Record*, 89 (1958); pp 153-70.

O'Rahilly, T.F., *The Two Patricks: A Lecture on the History of Christianity in Fifth-Century Ireland* (Dublin, 1942).

Ross, A., *Pagan Celtic Britain* (London, 1974).

Sharpe, R., 'St Patrick and the See of Armagh' in *Cambridge Medieval Celtic Studies*, 4 (1982); pp 33-59.

Stancliffe, C.E., 'Kings and Conversion: Some Comparisons between the Roman Mission and Patrick's to Ireland' in *Frühmittelalterliche Studien*, 14 (1980); pp 59-94.

Stokes, W. (ed. and trans.), *The Tripartite Life of Patrick, with other Documents Relating to that Saint* (2 vols. London, 1887).

Walsh, M. and Ó Cróinín, D. (eds), *Cummian's Letter De Controversia Paschali and the De Ratione Computandi* (Toronto, 1988).

Chapter Five: Irish Monasticism

Bieler, L. (ed. and trans.), *The Irish Penitentials* (Dublin, 1963; second edition, 1975).

De Paor, L., *Saint Patrick's World* (Blackrock, Co Dublin, 1993).

De Paor, L., 'The Aggrandisement of Armagh' in *Historical Studies*, 8 (1971); pp 95-110.

De Paor, M. and L., *Early Christian Ireland* (Dublin, 1958).

Hughes, K., *Early Christian Ireland: Introduction to the Sources* (London, 1972).

Hughes, K. and Hamlin, A., *The Modern Traveller to the Early Irish Church* (London, 1977).

Hughes, K., 'The Golden Age of Early Christian Ireland' in Moody, T.W. and Martin, F.X. (eds), *The Course of Irish History* (Cork, 1967); pp 76-90.

Kenney, J.F., *The Sources for the Early History of Ireland, Ecclesiastical: An Introduction and Guide* (New York, 1929; reprinted with additions by L. Bieler, Shannon, 1968; reissued Dublin, 1979).

Laing, L. and J., *Celtic Britain And Ireland, AD 200-800: The Myth of the Dark Ages* (Blackrock, Co Dublin, 1990).

Leask, H.G., *Irish Churches and Monastic Buildings* (2 vols. Dundalk, 1955).

MacDonald, A.D.S,, 'Aspects of the Monastery and Monastic Life in Adomnan's *Life of Columba*' in *Peritia*, 3 (1984); pp 271-302.

McGrath, F., *Education in Ancient and Medieval Ireland* (Dublin, 1979).

McNamara, M. (ed.), *Biblical Studies: The Medieval Irish Contribution* (Dublin, 1976).

Ó Fiaich, T., 'The Beginnings of Christianity' in Moody, T. W. and Martin F.X. (eds.), *The Course of Irish History* (Cork, 1967); pp 61-75.

Ryan, J., *Irish Monasticism: Origins and Early Development* (London, 1931; reissued New York, 1972).

BIBLIOGRAPHY AND REFERENCES

Ryan, J., 'The Monastic Institute' in Corish, P.J. (ed.), *A History of Irish Catholicism*, vol. 1, fasc. 2 (Dublin, 1972).

Walker, G.S.M. (ed. and trans.), *Sancti Columbani Opera* (Dublin, 1957).

Chapter Six: Some Famous Monastic Founders

Anderson, A.O. and M.O. (eds and trans.), *Adomnan's Life of Columba* (London, 1961).

Adamson, I., 'Selected Translations from the Bangor Antiphononary' in *Bangor: Light of the World* (Bangor, 1979).

Attwater, D., *Dictionary of Saints* (2nd edition: London, 1983).

Bede, 'In Esdram' in Migne, J.P. (ed.), *Patrologia Latina*, 91 (221 vols. Paris, 1844-64); col. 65.

Butler, A., Thurston, H. and Attwater, D, (eds and trans.), *The Lives of The Saints* (original edition appeared in 1756: 12 vols; London, 1926-38).

Cogitosus. Colgan, J. (ed.), *Triadis Thaumaturgae* (Louvain, 1647) and Migne, J.P. (ed.), *Patrologia Latina*, 62 (221 vols. Paris, 1844-64); col. 775 ff.

D'Arcy, M. Ryan, *The Saints of Ireland* (Cork, 1974).

De Paor, L., *Saint Patrick's World* (Blackrock, Co Dublin, 1993).

Farmer, D.H., *The Oxford Dictionary of Saints* (Oxford, 1982).

Herbert, M., *Iona, Kells, and Derry: The History and Hagiography of the Monastic 'Familia' of Columba* (Oxford, 1988).

Hughes, K., *Early Christian Ireland: Introduction to the Sources* (London, 1972).

Kenney, J.F., *The Sources for the Early History of Ireland, Ecclesiastical: An Introduction and Guide* (New York, 1929; reprinted with additions by L. Bieler, Shannon, 1968; reissued Dublin, 1979).

Mac Airt, S. and Mac Niocaill, G. (eds.), *The Annals of Ulster* (Dublin, 1983).

Mac Donald, A.D.S., 'Aspects of the Monastery and Monastic Life in Adoman's *Life of Columba*' in *Peritia*, 3 (1984); pp 271-302.

McCone, K., 'Brigit in the Seventh Century: A Saint With Three Lives?' in *Peritia*, 1 (1982); pp 107-45.

Mc Cone, K., 'An Introduction to Early Irish Saints' Lives' in *The Maynooth Review*, 11 (1984); pp 26-59.

Montague, H.P., *The Saints and Martyrs of Ireland* (Gerrards Cross, 1981).

Ryan, J., 'The Monastic Institute' in Corish, P.J. (ed.), *A History of Irish Catholicism*, vol. 1, fasc. 2 (Dublin, 1972).

Severin, T., *The Brendan Voyage* (London, 1978).

Smyth, A.P., *Warlords and Holy Men: Scotland, A.D. 80-1000* (London, 1984).

Stokes, W. (ed and trans), *Félire Óengusso Céli Dé: The Martyrology of Oengus the Culdee* (London, 1905).

Webb, J.F. (trans.), 'The Voyage of St Brendan' in Farmer, D.H. (ed.), *The Age of Bede* (London, 1983); pp 211-45.

Chapter Seven: Colum Cille

Anderson A.O. and M.O. (eds and trans.), *Adomnan's Life of Columba* (London, 1961).

Bede. Colgrave, B. and Mynors, R.A.B. (eds and trans.), *Bede's Ecclesiastical History of the English People* (Oxford, 1969).

Bannerman, J., 'The Dál Riata and Northern Ireland in the sixth and seventh centuries' in Carney, J. and Greene, D. (eds), *Celtic Studies: Essays in memory of Angus Matheson*, 1912-62 (London, 1969); pp 1-11.

Bowen, E. G., *Saints, Seaways and Settlements in the Celtic Lands* (Cardiff, 1969).

Byrne, F.J., 'The Ireland of St Columba' in *Historical Studies*, 5 (1965); pp 37-58.

Bullough, D.A., 'Columba, Adomnan and the Achievement of Iona' in *Scottish Historical Review*, 43 (1964).; pp 111-30: and 44 (1965); pp 17-33.

Bullough, D.A., 'The Missions to the English and Picts and their Heritage (to c.800)' in Lowe, H. (ed.), *Die Iren und Europa* (Stuttgart, 1982); pp 80-97.

Charles-Edwards, T.M., 'Bede, The Irish and The Britons' in *Celtica*, 15 (1983); pp 42-52.

Colum Cille (?), 'Altus Prosator' in Bernard, J.H. and Atkinson, R. (eds and trans), *The Irish Liber Hymnorum*, 1 (London, 1898); pp 62-89.

Colum Cille (?), 'Noli Pater' in Bernard, J.H. and Atkinson, (eds and trans.), *The Irish Liber Hymnorum*, 2 (London, 1898); pp 23-28 and 140-72.

Coyle, H.H., *Colum Cille* (Derry, 1975).

Dallán Forgaill. Kinsella, T. (trans.), 'A Poem in Praise of Colum Cille' in the *New Oxford Book of Irish Verse* (Oxford and New York, 1986).

Finlay, I., *Columba* (London, 1979).

Hale, R.B., *The Magnificent Gael* (Leominster, 1976).

Herbert, M., *Iona, Kells, and Derry: The History and Hagiography of the Monastic 'Familia' of Columba* (Oxford, 1988).

Hughes, K., *The Church in Early Irish Society* (London, 1966).

Kenney, J.F., *The Sources for the Early History of Ireland, Ecclesiastical: An Introduction and Guide* (New York, 1929; reprinted with additions by L. Bieler, Shannon, 1968; reissued Dublin, 1979).

Lacey, B., *Siege City: The Story of Derry and Londonderry* (Belfast, 1990).

Mac Airt, S. and Mac Niocaill, G. (eds and trans.), *The Annals of Ulster* (Dublin, 1983).

MacDonald, A. D. S., 'Aspects of the Monastery and Monastic Life in Adomnan's *Life of Columba*' in *Peritia*, 3 (1984); pp 271-302.

Mc Neill, J. T., *The Celtic Churches* (Chicago, 1974).

Marsden, J., *The Illustrated Columcille* (London, 1991).

Meehan, D. (ed.), *Adamnan's 'De Locis Sanctis'* (Dublin, 1958).

Menzies, L., *St Columba of Iona* (Glasgow, 1949).

Montague, H.P., *The Saints and Martyrs of Ireland* (Gerrards Cross, 1981).

Mould, D.D.C. Pochin, 'Naomh Colmcille' in *Irish Ecclesiastical Record*, 99 (1963); pp 381-91.

Ó Briain, F., 'The Expansion of Irish Christianity' in *Irish Historical Studies*, 3 (1942-3); pp 241-66: and 4 (1945-6); pp 131-63.

Reeves, W. (ed.), *The Life of St Columba, founder of Hy, written by Adamnan* (Dublin, 1857).

Schoel, C.G., *De ecclesiasticae Britonum Scottorumque historiae fontibus* (Berlin, 1851).

Simpson, W. Douglas, *The Historical Saint Columba* (Aberdeen, 1927).

Smyth, A.P., *Warlords and Holy Men: Scotland, A.D. 80-1000* (London, 1984).

Tunney, J., *Saint Colmcille and the Columban Heritage* (Gartan, Co Donegal, 1987).

Chapter Eight: Prominent Irish Saints in Britain

Attwater, D. *Dictionary of Saints* (2nd edition: London, 1983).

Bede. Colgrave, B. and Mynors, R.A.B. (eds and trans.), *Bede's Ecclesiastical History of the English People* (Oxford, 1969).

Bede. Webb, J.F. (trans.), 'Bede: Life of Cuthbert' in Farmer, D.H. (ed.), *The Age of Bede* (London, 1983); pp 41-102.

Anderson, M.O., 'Columba and other Irish Saints in Scotland' in *Historical Studies*, 5 (1965); pp 26-36.

Bowen, E.G., *Saints, Seaways and Settlements in the Celtic Lands* (Cardiff, 1969).

Bullough, D.A., 'The Missions to the English and Picts and their Heritage (to c.800)' in Lowe, H. (ed.), *Die Iren und Europa* (Stuttgart, 1982); pp 80-97.

D'Arcy, M. Ryan, *The Saints of Ireland* (Cork, 1974).

Duncan, A.A.M., 'Bede, Iona, and the Picts' in Davis, R.H.C. and Wallace-Hardrill, J.M. (eds.), *The Writing of History in the Middle Ages* (Oxford, 1981); pp 1-42.

Eddius Stephanus. Webb, J.F. (trans.), 'Eddius Stephanus: Life of Wilfrid' in Farmer, D.H. (ed.), *The Age of Bede* (London, 1983); pp 105-82.

Farmer, D.H., *The Oxford Dictionary of Saints* (Oxford, 1982).

Farmer, D.H. (trans.) 'Bede: Lives of the Abbots of Wearmouth and Jarrow' in Farmer, D.H. (ed.), *The Age of Bede* (London, 1983); pp 185-208.

Hughes, K., *The Church in Early Irish Society* (London, 1966).

Kenney, J.F., *The Sources for the Early History of Ireland, Ecclesiastical: An Introduction and Guide* (New York, 1929; reprinted with additions by L. Bieler, Shannon, 1968; reissued Dublin, 1979).

Leclercq, H., 'La Postérité Des Pénitentiels Insulaires' in *Dictionnaire d'archéologie et de liturgie*, t. 14 (1938), col. 244.

Mc Neill, J.T., *The Celtic Churches* (Chicago, 1974).

Marsden, J., *The Illustrated Columcille* (London, 1991).

Montague, H.P., *The Saints and Martyrs of Ireland* (Gerrards Cross, 1981).

Moran, P.F., *Irish Saints in Great Britain* (Dublin, 1879).

Ryan, J., 'Irish Missionary Work in Scotland and England' in Daniel-Rops, H. (ed.), *The Miracle of Ireland* (translated from the French by the Earl of Wicklow: Dublin, 1958).

Simpson, W. Douglas, *The Historical Saint Columba* (Aberdeen, 1927).

Simpson, W. Douglas, *The Celtic Church in Scotland* (Aberdeen, 1935).

Smyth, A.P., *Warlords and Holy Men: Scotland, A.D. 80-1000* (London, 1984).

Walahfrid Strabo. Joynt, M. (ed.) *The Life of St Gall* (London, 1927).

Chapter Nine: Columban and Other Peregrini

Anon., 'Life of Saint Valericus' in Krusch, B. (trans.) in *Monumenta Germaniae Historica. Scriptores Rerum Merovingicarum* 4 (Hanover and Liepzig, 1902); pp 157-75.

Bede. Colgrave, B. and Mynors, R.A.B. (eds and trans.), *Bede's Ecclesiastical History of the English People* (Oxford, 1969).

Berardis, V., *Italy and Ireland in the Middle Ages* (Dublin,1950).

Bowen, E.G., *Saints, Seaways and Settlements in the Celtic Lands* (Cardiff, 1969).

Concannon, H., *The Life of St Columban* (Dublin, 1915).

Charles-Edwards, T.M., 'The Social Background to Irish *peregrinatio'* in *Celtica,* 11 (1976); pp 43-59.

Daniel-Rops, H. (ed.), *The Miracle of Ireland* (translated from the French by the Earl of Wicklow; Dublin, 1959).

D'Arcy, M. Ryan, *The Saints of Ireland* (Cork, 1974).

Fredegarius. Wallace-Hadrill, J.M. (ed. and trans.), *The Fourth Book of the Chronicle of Fredegar* (London, 1960).

Gougaud, L., *Gaelic Pioneers of Christianity* (Dublin, 1923).

Gregory of Tours. Thorpe, L. (ed. and trans.), *The History of the Franks* (London, 1986).

James, E., 'Ireland and western Gaul in the Merovigian period' in Whitelock, D., McKitterick, R. and Dunville, D. (eds.), *Ireland in Early Medieval Europe* (Cambridge, 1982); pp 362-86.

Jonas. Krusch, B. (ed.), *Ionae Vitae Sanctorum Columbani, Vedastis, Johannis* (Hanover and Leipzig, 1905).

Kenney, J.F., *The Sources for the Early History of Ireland, Ecclesiastical: An Introduction and Guide* (New York, 1929; reprinted with additions by L. Bieler, Shannon, 1968; reissued Dublin, 1979).

Mc Neill, J.T., *The Celtic Churches* (Chicago, 1974).

Montague, H.P., *The Saints and Martyrs of Ireland* (Gerrards Cross, 1981).

Ó Briain, F., 'The Expansion of Irish Christianity' in *Irish Historical Studies,* 3 (1942-3) pp 241-66; and 4 (1945-6) pp 131-63.

Ó Fiaich, T., *Columbanus in his own words* (Dublin, 1974).

O'Mahony, D., *Irish Footprints on the Continent* (London, 1927).

Paulus Deaconus. Foulke, W.D. (ed. and trans.), *History of the Langobards* (London, 1907).

Tommasini, A., *Irish Saints in Italy* (translated by J.F. Scanlan; London, 1937).

Walahfrid Strabo. Joynt, M. (trans.), *The Life of St Gall* (London, 1927).

Walker, G.S.M. (ed. and trans.), *Sancti Columbani Opera,* (Dublin, 1957).

Chapter Ten: The Irish Penitentials

Bieler, L. (ed. and trans.), *The Irish Penitentials* (Dublin, 1963; second edition, 1975).

Bieler, L., 'Penitentials' in *New Catholic Encyclopedia,* 11 (New York, etc., 1967); pp 86-87.

Binchy, D.A. (trans.), 'The Old-Irish Penitential' and 'The Old-Irish Table of Commutations' in Bieler, L. (ed. and trans.), *The Irish Penitentials* (Dublin, 1963; second edition, 1975).

Brundage, J.A., *Law, Sex, and Christian Society in Medieval Europe* (Chicago, 1987).

Chadwick, N.K., *The Age of the Saints in the Early Celtic Church* (London, 1961).

Corish, P.J., 'The Pastoral Mission in the Early Irish Church' in *Léachtaí Cholm Cille*, 2 (1971); pp 14-25.

Hughes, K., *The Church in Early Irish Society* (London, 1966).

Hughes, K., *Early Christian Ireland: Introduction to the Sources* (London, 1972).

Kelly, F., *A Guide to Early Irish Law* (Dublin, 1988).

Leclercq, H., 'Pénitentiels' in *Dictionnaire d'archéologie et de liturgie*, t. 14 (1938); col. 215 ff.

Mac Airt, S. and Mac Niocaill, G. (eds and trans.), *The Annals of Ulster* (Dublin,1983).

Mc Neill, J.T. and Ganer, H.M., *Medieval Hand-books of Penance: A Translation of the Libri Poenitentialis and Selections from related Documents* (New York, 1938).

Palmer, P., 'Sacrament of Penance' in *New Catholic Encyclopedia*, 11 (New York, etc., 1967); pp 73-8.

Payer, P.J., *Sex and the Penitentials* (Toronto, 1984).

Plummer, C. (ed.), *'Venerabilis Baedae opera historica' tomus prior, prolegomena et textum continens* (Oxford, 1896).

Rule of Patrick (*Ríagail Pátraic*). O'Keeffe, J.F. (ed.), in *Ériu* 1 (1904); pp 216-24.

Ryan, J., *Irish Monasticism: Origins and Early Development* (London, 1931; reissued New York, 1972).

Sacred Congregation for Divine Worship, 'Decree Prot. n. 800/73' in *The Roman Ritual. The Rite of Penance* (revised by decree of the Second Vatican Ecumenical Council and published by authority of Pope Paul VI, Great Wakering, 1976); pp 5-6.

Wasserschleben, H. (ed.), *Die irische Kanonensammlung* (Leipzig, 1885).

Chapter Eleven: The Paschal Controversy

Bede. Colgrave, B. and Mynors, R.A.B. (eds. and trans.), *Bede's Ecclesiastical History of the English People* (Oxford, 1969).

Bede. Webb, J.F. (trans.), 'Bede: Life of Cuthbert' in Farmer, D.H. (ed.), *The Age of Bede* (London, 1983); pp 41-102.

Bullough, D.A., 'The Missions to the English and Picts and their Heritage (to c.800)' in Lowe, H. (ed.), *Die Iren und Europa* (Stuttgart, 1982); pp 80-97.

Charles-Edwards, T.M., 'Bede, The Irish And The Britons' in *Celtica*, 15 (1983); pp 42-52.

Corish, P.J., 'The Christian Mission' in Corish, P.J. (ed.), *A History of Irish Catholicism*, vol. 1, fasc. 3 (Dublin, 1972).

Corish, P.J., 'The Pastoral Mission In The Early Irish Church' in *Léachtaí Cholm Cille*, 2 (1971); pp 14-25.

Cummian, 'De controversia paschali' in Migne, J.P. (ed.), *Patrologia Latina*, 87 (221 vols. Paris, 1844-64); col. 969 ff.

Duncan, A.A.M., 'Bede, Iona, and the Picts' in Davis, R.H.C. and Wallace-Hadrill, J.M. (eds.), *The Writing of History in the Middle Ages* (Oxford, 1981); pp 1-42.

Eddius Stephanus. Webb, J.F. (trans.), 'Eddius Stephanus: Life of Wilfrid' in Farmer, D.H. (ed.), *The Age of Bede* (London, 1983); pp 105-82.

Harrison, K., 'Episodes in the history of Easter cycles in Ireland,' in Whitelock, D., McKitterick, R. and Dumville, D. (eds.), *Ireland In Early Medieval Europe* (Cambridge, 1982); pp 307-19.

Harrison, K., 'A Letter From Rome To The Irish Clergy, AD 640' in *Peritia*, 3 (1984); pp 222-29.

Hughes, K., *The Church in Early Irish Society* (London, 1966).

James, E., 'Bede And The Tonsure Question' in *Peritia*, 3 (1984); pp 85-98.

Kenney, J.E., *The Sources for the Early History of Ireland, Ecclesiastical: An Introduction and Guide* (New York, 1929; reprinted with additions by L. Bieler, Shannon, 1968; reissued Dublin, 1979).

Mc Neill, J.T., *The Celtic Churches* (Chicago, 1974).

Meissner, J.L., Gough, *The Celtic Church in England* (London, 1929).

Smyth, A.P., *Warlords and Holy Men, Scotland, A.D. 80-1000* (London, 1984).

Walsh, M. and Ó Cróinín, D. (eds), *Cummian's Letter De Controversia Paschali and the De Ratione Computandi* (Toronto, 1988).

Chapter Twelve: Celtic Church Art

De Paor, M. and L., *Early Christian Ireland* (London, 1958).

Hamlin, A. (ed.), *Historic Monuments of Northern Ireland* (Belfast, 1983).

Harbinson, P., *Guide to the National Monuments in the Republic of Ireland* (Dublin, 1979).

Haseloff, G., 'Insular Animal Styles with Special Reference to Irish Art in the Early Medieval Period' in Ryan, M. (ed.), *Ireland and Insular Art A.D. 500-1200* (Dublin, 1987); pp 45-55.

Henry, F., *Early Christian Irish Art* (Dublin, 1954).

Henry, F., *Irish Art in the early Christian period* (to A.D. 800) (London, 1965).

Hughes, K., *Early Christian Ireland: Introduction to the Sources* (London, 1972).

Hughes, K. and Hamlin, A., *The Modern Traveller to the Early Irish Church*, (London, 1977).

Laing, L. and J., *Celtic Britain And Ireland, AD 200-800: The Myth of the Dark Ages* (Blackrock, Co Dublin, 1990).

Leask, H.G., *Irish Churches and Monastic Buildings* (2 vols. Dundalk, 1955).

Mitchell, G.F., 'Foreign Influences and the Beginnings of Christian Art' in Mitchell, G.F. et alii, *Treasures of Irish Art 1500 B.C.-1500 A.D.* (New York, 1977); pp 54-92.

Ó Carragáin, E., 'The Ruthwell Cross and Irish High Crosses: Some Points of Comparison and Contrast' in Ryan, M. (ed.) *Ireland and Insular Art A.D.500-1200* (Dublin, 1987); pp 118-28.

Ó Cróinín, D., 'Merovingian Politics and Insular Calligraphy: The Historical Background to the Book of Durrow and Related Manuscripts' in Ryan, M. (ed.), *Ireland and Insular Art A.D.500-1200* (Dublin, 1987); pp 40-3.

Ó Floinn, D., *The Integral Irish Tradition* (Dublin, 1968).

Roth, U., 'Early Insular Manuscripts: Ornament and Archaeology, with Special Reference to the Dating of the Book of Durrow' in Ryan, M. (ed.) *Ireland and Insular Art A.D.500-1200* (Dublin, 1987); pp 66-74.

Ryan, M., *Treasures of Ireland: Irish Art, 3000 B.C.-1500 A.D.* (Dublin, 1983).

Rynne, E., 'The Date of the Ardagh Chalice' in Ryan, M. (ed.), *Ireland and Insular Art A.D.500-1200* (Dublin, 1987); pp 85-9.